Christina Calveley entered journalism on leaving
school at the age of sixteen and worked for several
years on local newspapers before deciding to
enter trade journalism. She worked on a number
of leading trade magazines and became a freelance journalist in 1978. As a freelance she has
continued her association with trade magazines
and writes for several specialist journals. She has
also written *The Family Quiz Book* published by
Penguin in 1980.

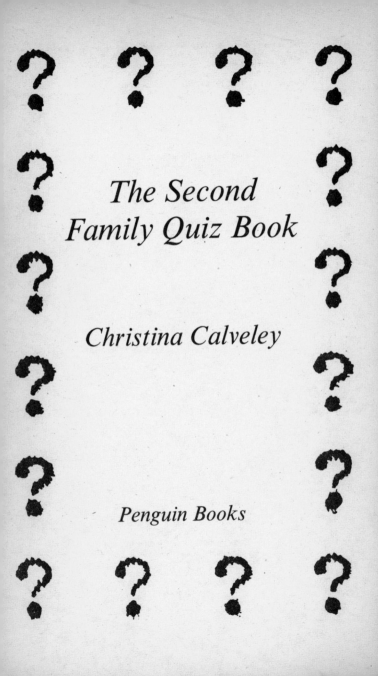

The Second Family Quiz Book

Christina Calveley

Penguin Books

Penguin Books Ltd, Harmondsworth, Middlesex, England
Penguin Books, 625 Madison Avenue, New York, New York 10022, U.S.A.
Penguin Books Australia Ltd, Ringwood, Victoria, Australia
Penguin Books Canada Ltd, 2801 John Street, Markham, Ontario, Canada L3R 1B4
Penguin Books (N.Z.) Ltd, 182–190 Wairau Road, Auckland 10, New Zealand

—

First published 1982

—

Copyright © Christina Calveley, 1982
All rights reserved

—

Printed and bound in Great Britain by
Cox & Wyman Ltd, Reading
Filmset in Monophoto Times Roman by
Northumberland Press Ltd, Gateshead, Tyne and Wear

To Stephen

with all my love and thanks

AUTHOR'S NOTE

To all readers who read and enjoyed my first *Family Quiz Book* I should like to say that I hope they find this further set of 800 questions and answers equally enjoyable. In these pages you will find many new subjects, from Romans and Greeks to Rugby, TV and Radio to Untimely Ends, none of which were in the first book. At the same time, many of the sections which proved particularly popular in that book, such as Films and Film Stars, Literature and Sporting Knowledge, have been retained with a whole new set of questions. I have also included a further section on General Knowledge.

To all new readers I should like to say that I hope they will spend happy hours trying to answer the questions and that they will find many sections of particular interest to them.

In compiling this second book I have been grateful for the assistance, suggestions and ideas from a number of my friends, and I should like to place on record a special word of thanks to Stephen Mitchell, Michael Hall and Malcolm Bowen for their help.

CONTENTS

Questions

1.
GENERAL KNOWLEDGE (I)

1. Who were Neil Armstrong's two companions on the Apollo XI moonship landing on the moon?

2. How do you convert a temperature on the Centigrade scale to one on the Fahrenheit scale?

3. What is the more common name for Aurora Borealis?

4. In which months do the following full moons occur: (a) Harvest (b) Hunter's?

5. What animal is the symbol of the World Wildlife Fund?

6. With which comedians are the following catchphrases usually associated: (a) Hullo, playmates! (b) How tickled I am! (c) Nick, nick, nick?

7. What are male and female swans called?

8. Whereabouts is the Sea of Tranquillity located?

9. Which stone, discovered in Egypt and now in the British Museum, enabled scientists to decipher Egyptian hieroglyphics?

10. What are the flora and fauna of a region?

11. Only one of the original Seven Wonders of the World still survives. Which is it?

12. What was created by the Treaty of Rome in 1957?

13. Where does the International Court of Justice have its headquarters?

14. What are the monetary units of the following countries: (*a*) France (*b*) Germany (*c*) Denmark (*d*) Greece (*e*) Portugal?

15. Where in England is the headquarters of the Open University?

16. Who designed the Houses of Parliament in London between 1840 and 1846?

17. What is a geyser?

18. In which country was the explorer and mountaineer Sir Edmund Hillary born?

19. When was the Festival of Britain held, to show the world the recovery which the UK had made from the Second World War?

20. Which city was the capital of Ptolemaic Egypt?

2.
TV AND RADIO

1. In which TV series do the following characters appear and who play the parts: (*a*) Elsie Tanner (*b*) Sue-Ellen Ewing (*c*) Hawkeye (*d*) Jack Ford?

2. Who play the roles of Jonathan and Jennifer Hart in the TV series *Hart to Hart*?

3. When did the BBC first begin making regular TV transmissions?

4. In which long-running radio serial does the character Tom Forrest appear and who plays him?

5. Who play the following TV detectives: (*a*) Starsky and Hutch (*b*) Kojak (*c*) Steve McGarrett?

6. The title of the radio show *ITMA* was an acronym based on a catch phrase. What did *ITMA* stand for?

7. Which two actors have played the role of Simon Templar in the TV series, *The Saint*?

8. Who was Director-General of the BBC from its formation in 1922 until 1938?

9. Who is the quizmaster in these TV programmes: (*a*) *Mastermind* (*b*) *University Challenge* (*c*) *Sale of the Century*?

10. Who was the first woman to read the news nationally on TV?

11. In which TV series do Bodie and Doyle appear and who play the roles?

12. Who used the phrase 'Goodnight and I love you all' as a sign-off line during a series of the *Morecambe and Wise Show* on BBC TV?

13. What is the profession of Eddie Shoestring in the TV series *Shoestring* and who plays the role?

14. Which female TV personality is presenter of *That's Life*?

15. With which TV variety show is Leonard Sachs associated?

16. Who introduced Kaptain Kremmen to the radio and, later, to TV?

17. Which three British radio stations were replaced by BBC Radios One, Two, Three and Four?

18. Who played the roles of George and Mildred in the TV comedy series of that name?

19. With which TV programmes are the following catchphrases associated: (*a*) And now for something completely different! (*b*) Bernie, the bolt! (*c*) I didn't get where I am today ... (*d*) I'm free! (*e*) It's good-night from me/And it's good-night from him! (*f*) Kissy, kissy!?

20. With which radio programmes are the following catchphrases associated: (*a*) Can I do you now, sir? (*b*) Don't some mothers have 'em (*c*) Left hand down a bit (*d*) Sur le telephoneo (*e*) Ying-tong-iddle-i-po!?

3.
UNTIMELY ENDS

1. Which poet and dramatist was stabbed to death at a tavern in Deptford, London, in 1593?

2. How and where did King William II of England die?

3. Which Florentine religious reformer was crucified before the crowd in the Piazza della Signoria and then burned on 23 May 1498?

4. Where did Davy Crockett die in 1836?

5. How did politician and philosopher Francis Bacon die in 1626?

6. Which of Henry VIII's wives were executed?

7. Who shot Lee Harvey Oswald, the alleged assassin of President Kennedy?

8. How did UN Secretary-General Dag Hammarskjöld die in 1961?

9. Which famous pop musician was shot dead outside his New York apartment in 1980?

10. Who became the first Christian martyr, being stoned to death in around AD 36?

11. Eight members of which conspiracy were tried on 27 January 1606 and executed on 30 and 31 January 1606?

12. How did George Villiers, first Duke of Buckingham, die in 1628?

13. Who was beheaded at Fotheringay Castle on 8 February 1587?

14. How did King Richard I of England die?

15. Who said of his death by execution: 'This is sharp medicine, but it is a sure cure for all diseases'?

16. How did T. E. Lawrence, author of *Seven Pillars of Wisdom*, die in 1935?

17. Which two bishops were burnt at the stake on 16 October 1555?

18. How did Nazi leader Hermann Goering cheat the gallows?

19. Where was General Charles Gordon killed in 1885?

20. How did the artist Vincent van Gogh die in 1890?

4.
THE OLYMPIC GAMES

1. British middle-distance runners Steve Ovett and Sebastian Coe both won gold medals at the 1980 Summer Olympics. In which events?

2. In which two events did Alberto Juantoreno win gold medals at the 1976 Olympics?

3. When and where did the first modern Olympiad take place and how many nations took part?

4. Which countries did the following Olympic gold-medal winners represent: (*a*) Frank Shorter (*b*) John Walker (*c*) Hasely Crawford (*d*) Don Quarrie (*e*) Valery Borzov?

5. Who won Britain's only gold medal at the 1980 Winter Olympic Games?

6. What happened to runner Lasse Viren in the 10,000 metres race at the 1972 Olympics?

7. Which winner of five Olympic gold medals was voted 'greatest swimmer of the half-century' by 250 sports writers in 1950?

8. Who was the first man to win the Olympic marathon twice and for which country did he compete?

9. Where were the Summer Olympic Games held in: (*a*) 1936 (*b*) 1968 (*c*) 1980?

10. In which event did Briton Daley Thompson win a gold medal at the 1980 Summer Olympics?

11. Which new event was added to the 1980 Winter Olympics?

12. Who won four gold medals – 100 metres, 200 metres, 4 × 100 metres relay and long jump – at the 1936 Olympics?

13. Skier Jean-Claude Killy won three gold medals at the 1968 Winter Olympics. In which events?

14. In which years have the Summer Olympics been held in London?

15. Who won the decathlon title in 1948 when he was only seventeen years old and successfully defended the crown four years later – the only man to retain this championship?

16. In which event did Allan Wells win the gold medal at the 1980 Olympics? Who beat him in his other event?

17. Where were the Winter Olympics held in: (a) 1968 (b) 1976 (c) 1980?

18. What did Teofilio Stevenson achieve at the 1972, 1976 and 1980 Olympics?

19. In which sports have the following won Olympic gold medals: (a) Mark Spitz (b) Nelli Kim (c) George Foreman (d) Alexandr Voronin?

20. At the 1976 Olympics which gymnast became the first to be awarded a perfect score in Olympic competition and which country was she representing?

5.
INDUSTRIAL HISTORY

1. What device did John Kay invent in 1733 to speed the process of weaving?

2. Which of Isambard Kingdom Brunel's steamships was the first to operate a scheduled transatlantic service?

3. For what purpose was a steam engine, invented by James Watt, installed at Whitbread's Brewery in London in 1775 and what did it replace?

4. What invention did Thomas Newcomen patent in 1705?

5. In 1778 which English engineer designed the first flush water closet to be manufactured in quantity, the same man having also invented a lock which is still used today?

6. Who invented the following: (*a*) spinning frame (*b*) spinning jenny (*c*) spinning mule?

7. In which year was the Great Exhibition held in Hyde Park, London, under the patronage of Prince Albert?

8. Who first introduced coke fuel for iron-smelting in place of charcoal in 1709?

9. Why did Josiah Wedgwood finance the cutting of canals in Britain?

10. Who was the Cornishman who first constructed a steam loco-motive and displayed it, running round a circular track, at Euston in 1809?

11. What did Edmund Cartwright invent in 1784 which enabled weaving to catch up with spinning?

12. Who were the Charles Stewart and Henry who formed a partnership in 1906 to produce British cars?

13. Where was the world's first cast-iron bridge erected in 1777?

14. In what year was the Factory Act forbidding the employment of children under nine years old passed in Britain?

15. Who were the Luddites?

16. With whom did James Watt go into partnership in 1774?

17. What was 'Puffing Billy', which was introduced by William Hedley in 1813 at Wylam, Northumberland?

18. Why did the firm of Fry's invest in a steam engine in 1798?

19. Which Yorkshire railway promoter, who made and lost a fortune between 1836 and 1849, was known as the 'Railway King'?

20. What contribution did Henry Cort make to the forging side of the iron industry in 1784?

6.
WRITERS

1. Who wrote *Gerald: A Portrait* as a biography of her father?

2. What do the following writers' initials stand for: (*a*) G. K. Chesterton (*b*) D. H. Lawrence (*c*) C. P. Snow (*d*) J. M. Barrie?

3. Whose real name was Josef Korzeniowski?

4. What were the Christian names of the three Brontë sisters and their brother?

5. Under what pseudonym did Mary Ann Evans write?

6. Who wrote *Silent Spring* as an indictment of the use of poisonous chemicals by farmers?

7. What nationality are or were the following: (*a*) Hans Christian Andersen (*b*) Samuel Beckett (*c*) Bertolt Brecht (*d*) Alexandre Dumas (*e*) Maxim Gorky (*f*) Franz Kafka?

8. Under what pseudonym did Sir William Neil Conner write for the *Daily Mirror* for many years?

9. Who described the delights of angling and the English countryside in *The Compleat Angler*?

10. What relation is writer Monica Dickens to Charles Dickens?

11. Who wrote in his diary: 'Home, and, being washing-day, dined upon cold meat'?

12. Where was George Orwell born and what career did he pursue from 1922 to 1927?

13. Which famous detective writer has also written 'straight' fiction under the pseudonym of Mary Westmacott?

14. Where is Rudyard Kipling buried?

15. Which twentieth-century dramatist claimed to write for a mythical, middle-class member of the audience, 'Aunt Edna', a lady of conventional outlook?

16. What was Saki's real name?

17. Which two dramatists have collaborated to write a number of plays including *England, Our England*, *All Things Bright and Beautiful* and *Say Who You Are*?

18. Who was the famous French novelist who was in the Resistance during the war, played soccer and died in a car accident in 1960?

19. Which two writers, members of the Bloomsbury Group, founded the Hogarth Press in 1917?

20. Who wrote under the pseudonym of 'Q'?

7.
AMERICA AND AMERICANS

1. From 1933 to 1963 which rocky island in San Francisco Bay was used as a prison for long-term criminals?

2. What are the capitals of the following states: (a) Arkansas (b) Georgia (c) Texas (d) Nevada?

3. Who became president of the USA after the assassination of John F. Kennedy in 1963?

4. When was prohibition of alcohol introduced in America?

5. In 1950 which American senator claimed that the State Department was harbouring 205 communists?

6. Which American mountain region contains three famous national parks – Yosemite, Sequoia and King's Canyon?

7. Who is the only American president to have served more than two terms in office and between what years did he serve?

8. In 1836 which Texan fort was defended by 183 guards against the Mexicans, all the guards being killed?

9. Which US states are popularly known as the following: (a) Bluegrass (b) Evergreen (c) Green Mountain (d) Mormon?

10. Where was former US Secretary of State, Henry Kissinger, born?

11. What was Cape Canaveral, site of the USAF Missile Test Centre, renamed in 1963, reverting to its former name in 1973?

12. Who was Phineas Taylor Barnum who lived from 1810 to 1891?

13. Where in America is the famous Rose Bowl where pageants, football matches, etc., are held?

14. Who became director of the FBI in 1921 and what does FBI stand for?

15. In 1972 who became the first American to become official world champion in chess and whom did he defeat to win the title?

16. Which is the largest – and oldest – national park in the US?

17. Which American Confederate army officer was known as 'Stonewall'?

18. What is West Point in Newburgh, south-east New York?

19. Who were the two brothers who led the notorious Quantril gang which terrorized the Midwest in the 1870s?

20. From whom did America purchase Alaska in 1867?

8.

TRANSPORT

1. What name was given to Henry Ford's first make of car?

2. Who was Britain's first major canal-builder – his first project being a canal to carry coal from the Duke of Bridgewater's mines at Worsley to Manchester?

3. What is a bathyscaphe?

4. Who made the first transatlantic flight in 1919?

5. The first nuclear-powered submarine was launched by the US Navy in 1954. What was it called?

6. What contribution did Scottish engineer John McAdam make to modern road construction?

7. For whom was the first purpose-built bomber aircraft made?

8. Which was the first airline to use aeroplanes rather than Zeppelins?

9. Where was the world's first traffic signal installed in 1868?

10. Which Lancashire inventor devised the modern 'catseye' stud for roads?

11. In 1928 who became the first woman to make a solo Atlantic flight?

12. What did Jean Pierre Blanchard and Dr John J. Jeffries achieve in 1785?

13. In 1886 which two German engineers put the first practical motorcars on the road?

14. Which two British airlines were amalgamated in 1972 to form British Airways?

15. In which cities are the following airports: (*a*) John F. Kennedy (*b*) Orly (*c*) Haneda?

16. Which motorcar company was built up by Viscount William Nuffield?

17. Who built the first rigid-frame airship in 1900?

18. Which was the first supersonic airliner and in what year did it make its first flight?

19. What did Wiley Post achieve in 1933?

20. For what were the Montgolfier brothers, Joseph Michel and Jacques Etienne, famous in the eighteenth century?

9.
FOOD AND DRINK

1. With which countries are the following dishes normally associated: (*a*) Moussaka (*b*) Goulash (*c*) Pizza (*d*) Chop suey (*e*) Beef stroganoff (*f*) Paella?

2. What is lava bread which is eaten in South Wales?

3. Which liqueur was originated by Carthusian monks?

4. What is a 'bouquet garni'?

5. In which country would you eat a 'knacker' and what is it?

6. What drink is sometimes called 'Cactus Whisky'?

7. From which countries do the following cheeses come: (*a*) Gorgonzola (*b*) Gouda (*c*) Gruyère?

8. What are 'croutons'?

9. From which animals do (*a*) veal and (*b*) venison come?

10. What do anisette and pernod have in common?

11. Which two liquors have historically been used in the making of an egg-nog?

12. From which country does 'Apfelstrudel' come?

13. In which country did gin originate?

14. From which part of the ox do we get tripe?

15. What is 'grenadine'?

16. What type of flour is used by Jews in cooking for the celebration of the Passover?

17. Which country do Angostura Bitters come from?

18. From which fruits are (*a*) Maraschino and (*b*) Slivovitz made?

19. In which country might you eat from a 'smorgasbord' and what is it?

20. With which countries are these soups usually associated: (*a*) Bird's nest (*b*) Minestrone (*c*) Kaisersuppe?

10.
RECORD SETTERS

1. Who, in 1978, set a record for holding the world heavyweight boxing championship for the shortest period of time – just 212 days?

2. Which painting was assessed for insurance purposes at the highest-ever figure of $100,000,000 (then £35.7 million) in 1962?

3. Who broke the land-speed record in 1935 and the water-speed record four years later?

4. In which sport did Vasili Alexeyev of the USSR break a total of eighty official world records between 24 January 1970 and 1 November 1977?

5. Who were the three members of Apollo X which, on its trans-Earth return flight on 26 May 1969, reached a speed of 24,791 mph, the fastest speed at which humans had ever travelled?

6. In 1976 which snooker player became the first ever to make a '16 red' clearance with a break of 146?

7. Who is the only world heavyweight boxing champion to have been undefeated during his professional career which spanned the years 1947–56?

8. Which is the world's most widely distributed book?

9. What record was set up by footballer Paul Allen when he played for West Ham United in an FA Cup Final against Arsenal on 10 May 1980?

10. Who, on 17 December 1979, set up the highest speed ever achieved on land at Edwards Air Force Base, California, and what was the name of his rocket-engined car?

11. Which poem by Rudyard Kipling is believed to be the most translated in the world?

12. During an England *v* Colombia soccer match on 20 May 1970, who scored his 49th international goal – a career record for England?

13. In 1979 tennis player Billie-Jean King broke the record for the number of Wimbledon titles won by a woman. How many had she won?

14. What record did Valeriy Ryumin and Vladimir Lyakhov set up between 25 February 1979 and 19 August 1979?

15. Which singer drew the largest-ever audience – estimated at 175,000 – to his solo performance at the Maracana Stadium, Rio de Janeiro, on 26 January 1980?

16. On 18 July 1951 who became the oldest man – at over thirty-seven years of age – to win the world heavyweight boxing crown?

17. Who has won a record number of film Oscars, comprising twenty statuettes and nine other plaques and certificates?

18. Which American male swimmer has won the greatest number of Olympic gold medals, and how many did he win?

19. A world heavyweight boxing champion held the title for 11 years 252 days – a record for all boxing divisions. Who was he?

20. Which British novelist had 564 books published under his own name and thirteen *noms de plume* between 1932 and his death in 1973?

11.

GREEKS AND ROMANS

1. Who was the Macedonian king who conquered the Athenians, and who was his son?

2. At which naval battle did Augustus defeat Mark Antony and Cleopatra?

3. Which mountain is sacred to Dionysus, Apollo and the Muses?

4. Which Roman Emperor built a wall to protect England from the Picts and Scots?

5. Which feat does the Olympic marathon commemorate?

6. Who was proclaimed emperor of Rome by the Praetorian Guard after the murder of Caligula?

7. What ancient sites did these two archaeologists discover (*a*) Heinrich Schliemann (*b*) Arthur Evans?

8. Which member of the first Roman triumvirate was defeated by Caesar at Pharsala, and what happened to him?

9. Who were the Greeks and Romans who wrote the following histories: (*a*) History of the Persian Wars (*b*) From the Beginning of the City (*c*) Histories, Annals, Germania (*d*) History of the Peloponnesian War?

10. Which Roman emperor ruled alone after murdering his brother Geta?

11. In the wake of Alexander the Great a Hellenistic ruler began a dynasty in Egypt. Who was he and who was the last in the line?

12. Julius Caesar's action in crossing which river was tantamount to a declaration of war against Pompey and the Senate?

13. Which were the principal Greek states fighting in the Peloponnesian War?

14. With whom did Mark Antony form a triumvirate to defeat the murderers of Julius Caesar and rule the Roman Empire?

15. Who wrote the following (a) *Seven Against Thebes* (b) *Oedipus Rex* (c) *The Frogs*?

16. Which Roman emperor arranged the deaths of his heir Britannicus, his mother Agrippina, his wives Octavia and Poppaea, and many others?

17. Pictured in a famous piece of pottery fighting a lion, he ruled Athens from 443 to 429 BC. Who was he?

18. Who was chosen as Roman emperor by his troops while campaigning in Palestine in AD 69, and what famous structure did he have built?

19. Which Athenian, appointed archon in 594 BC, eliminated debts on landed property?

20. Who was the first Roman emperor to become a Christian?

12.
TWENTIETH-CENTURY LITERATURE

1. Who wrote the following: (*a*) *How Green Was My Valley* (*b*) *Brideshead Revisited* (*c*) *The Quiet American* (*d*) *The Inheritors* (*e*) *The Dogs of War* (*f*) *The Magus*?

2. What was the sequel to John Braine's novel *Room at the Top*?

3. By what collective name are the following novels known and who wrote them: *Justine, Balthazar, Mountolive* and *Clea*?

4. In whose novels does the private detective Slim Callaghan appear?

5. Who wrote the following plays: (*a*) *The Quare Fellow* (*b*) *Arsenic and Old Lace* (*c*) *Arms and the Man* (*d*) *The Constant Wife* (*e*) *Blithe Spirit* (*f*) *The Crucible*?

6. Of which novel is 'The Illuminating Diary of a Professional Lady' the subtitle, and who wrote it?

7. Which novel by Kingsley Amis was filmed in 1962 as *Only Two Can Play*?

8. Whose experiences of near destitution in Paris and later as a tramp in England gave him the material for his book, *Down and Out in Paris and London*?

9. In which of John Osborne's plays do these characters appear: (*a*) Jimmy Porter (*b*) Archie Rice?

10. Which novel by Somerset Maugham tells of a club-footed failed artist turned medical student?

11. Who taught Eliza Doolittle to speak pure English in Shaw's play *Pygmalion*?

12. Which two novels by Arnold Bennett completed the trilogy started by *Clayhanger*?

13. In which novels do the following characters appear and who created them: (*a*) Holden Caulfield (*b*) Pinkie (*c*) Gandalf (*d*) Yossarian?

14. Which two famous English writers travelled to China in 1938 on the eve of the Second World War and, as a result, wrote a book called *Journey To A War*?

15. To what group of people did Rudyard Kipling give the name 'Janeites' in a story of that title?

16. Who wrote the trilogy of novels entitled *Sword of Honour*, and what were the titles of the three books?

17. In which two novels by D. H. Lawrence do Ursula and Gudrun Brangwen appear?

18. The following books have been turned into films: who wrote them: (*a*) *The Thirty-nine Steps* (*b*) *A Clockwork Orange* (*c*) *Breakfast at Tiffany's* (*d*) *Death on the Nile* (*e*) *The African Queen* (*f*) *Jaws*?

19. Which popular character was created by W. E. Johns in his children's books?

20. In which of E. M. Forster's novels does the Herriton family appear?

13.
MYTH,
LEGEND AND FOLKLORE

1. Who founded a state in Cappadocia, Asia Minor, from which all men were excluded?

2. In the legend of King Arthur, what was the Holy Grail?

3. Who was condemned by the Olympians to stand at the western edge of the earth, supporting the heavens on his head and shoulders?

4. In Egyptian mythology, who was Anubis?

5. Which villain of European folktales was the subject of a story written by Charles Perrault in 1697?

6. For what is 'banshee' the Irish or Scottish name?

7. Who were the Greek gods of: (*a*) wine (*b*) love (*c*) the sea?

8. Which fictional villain was probably based on Prince Vlad III of Wallachia in Romania, who lived from 1431 to 1477?

9. Who was the wizard who advised King Arthur?

10. In mythology, what was El Dorado?

11. Which king of Phrygia was famous for being able to turn everything he touched into gold?

12. Who were the Roman gods of (*a*) fire (*b*) the vine (*c*) war?

13. According to legend, who was forced by the tyrannical Austrian viceroy Gessler to shoot an apple off his son's head?

14. In Greek mythology, what was a 'sphinx'?

15. Which king of Ithaca devised the ruse of the wooden horse of Troy?

16. What is the more popular name for All Saints' Eve and on which day of the year is it observed?

17. Which Archbishop of Canterbury was credited with inventing the magic power of horseshoes?

18. In Irish folklore, what can leprechauns be forced to reveal – provided that, having caught them, one never takes one's eyes off them?

19. Who were the wives of (*a*) Zeus (*b*) Jupiter?

20. How many labours were imposed on the Greek hero Heracles by Eurystheus?

14.
GENERAL KNOWLEDGE (II)

1. Which language is spoken by more people in the world than any other?

2. What unit of speed is equivalent to one nautical mile per hour?

3. Which Pacific island was occupied in 1790 by mutineers from HMS *Bounty*?

4. In which year (*a*) was the first man launched into space (*b*) did the first men land on the moon?

5. After Australia, which is the largest island in the world?

6. What is a knoll?

7. Charlie Brown, Linus and Snoopy are cartoon characters in which comic strip, and who created them?

8. What is recorded on a seismograph?

9. In 1972, which former Rhodesian Prime Minister was imprisoned in Rhodesia and kept in solitary confinement without trial?

10. What is the difference between a stalactite and a stalagmite?

11. Who invented the revolver in 1835?

12. What are the young of the following called: (*a*) Goose (*b*) Owl (*c*) Frog (*d*) Cod?

13. By whom did Cleopatra of Egypt bear a son, Caesarion, who later became Ptolemy XIV?

14. What derisive title was given by British listeners to William Joyce, who broadcast Nazi propaganda from Germany during the Second World War, and what happened to him at the end of the war?

15. Which are (*a*) the largest sea and (*b*) the largest gulf in the world?

16. What type of eagle is the emblem of the USA?

17. The measurement, the yard, was originally said to be the distance between which two points?

18. What is the Russian equivalent of an American astronaut?

19. What colours are the flags of the following countries: (*a*) Eire (*b*) Belgium (*c*) Austria (*d*) France?

20. Which famous nun won the Nobel Peace Prize in 1979?

15.
NATURAL HISTORY

1. Which are the two most common birds in Britain?

2. What is (*a*) a 'covert' and (*b*) a 'covey'?

3. 'Black-beetle' is a popular but inaccurate name for which British insect?

4. Which is the largest carnivorous mammal in Britain?

5. For what is 'brisling' a fisherman's term?

6. What do the following societies study: (*a*) British Bryological Society (*b*) British Herpetological Society (*c*) British Mycological Society (*d*) British Pteridological Society?

7. Where do swallows and cuckoos migrate to in winter?

8. What name is given to the albino domesticated form of the polecat, and what is it used for hunting?

9. Which is the only native British mammal that truly hibernates?

10. What is (*a*) Devil's coach-horse (*b*) Devil's Fingers?

11. In Scotland what is a 'corrie'?

12. What is measured on the Beaufort Scale?

13. Why is the Cardinal Spider so called?

14. What is a 'beck'?

15. During the first year of its life, what is the young of the fallow deer called?

16. What does 'fraying' mean?

17. Jack, doe and leveret are the male, female and young of which animal?

18. Which is the largest type of wasp in the UK?

19. Of what are (a) Camberwell Beauty and (b) Kentish Glory species?

20. When a stoat is in its white winter pelage what is it called?

16.
FILMS
AND FILM STARS

1. In which film did Humphrey Bogart use the phrase 'Here's looking at you, kid'?

2. What was Marilyn Monroe's real name?

3. Which Walt Disney cartoon character made his debut in the film *Steamboat Willie*?

4. Who played the leading male and female roles in the film *Brief Encounter*, and who directed it?

5. Of which Thomas Hardy novel has Roman Polanski made a film and what is it called?

6. In which film did James Dean make his screen debut?

7. Who is associated with the phrase 'I want to be alone'?

8. Which two gold medallists from the 1924 Olympic Games are the subject of the film *Chariots of Fire*?

9. Who directed the following films: (*a*) *The Deer Hunter* (*b*) *Annie Hall* (*c*) *Oliver* (*d*) *Midnight Cowboy* (*e*) *From Here to Eternity* (*f*) *Exodus*?

10. In the 1968 Oscars, Katherine Hepburn and Barbra Streisand tied for the Best Actress award. Which films did they receive their award for?

11. Who played the title role in the film *The Godfather*?

12. The Barrymores were two brothers and one sister who were famous stage and film actors. What were their Christian names?

13. Which German actress's real name was Maria Magdalene von Kosch, and in which film did she make her debut in 1930?

14. Who played the two reporters, Woodward and Bernstein, in the film *All the President's Men*?

15. In which film did Clark Gable say 'Frankly, my dear, I don't give a damn'?

16. Which boxer was portrayed in the film *Raging Bull*, and who played the role?

17. Who played the title roles in the film *Butch Cassidy and the Sundance Kid*?

18. Who was named best actor or best actress in the Oscar awards for the following films: (*a*) *Cabaret* (*b*) *The Goodbye Girl* (*c*) *The French Connection* (*d*) *Klute* (*e*) *In the Heat of the Night* (*f*) *Mary Poppins*?

19. Whom did American film actress Grace Kelly marry?

20. Who played the Cincinnati Kid in the film of that name?

17.
RUGBY

Rugby Union

1. Which two national sides contest Rugby Union's Calcutta Cup?

2. Where are the headquarters of the Rugby Unions for (*a*) Wales (*b*) Scotland (*c*) Ireland?

3. Which is the oldest Rugby Union club in existence, dating from 1843?

4. At which Paris stadium does the French national team play most of its international Rugby Union matches?

5. In which countries do teams compete for (*a*) Ranfurly Shield (*b*) Currie Cup?

6. Which Rugby Union stars were given the following nicknames and from which countries did they come: (*a*) Pinetree (*b*) Mighty Mouse (*c*) The Golden Boy (*d*) The Boot?

7. Who, in his last game on 4 May 1976, scored his 312th try for Llanelli, a British club rugby record?

8. Which national Rugby Union side celebrated its centenary in 1981?

9. Who captained the English Rugby Union side which won the international championship in 1980?

10. For which national sides do or did the following Rugby Union stars play: (*a*) Mike Gibson (*b*) Andy Irvine (*c*) Phil Bennett (*d*) Tony Neary?

Rugby League

1. Which Rugby League side won its first ever Challenge Cup in 1980?

2. Who scored a record number of 221 goals in Rugby League in the 1972–3 season, and for which club was he playing?

3. Which club won the Rugby League Challenge Cup ten times between 1910 and 1978?

4. In June 1980 a record transfer fee of £40,000 was paid for Rugby League player Trevor Skerrett. Which two clubs were involved?

5. Who captained Wigan a record six times in the Rugby League Cup Finals between 1958 and 1966?

6. Which London soccer club set up a Rugby League side which played in the second division for the first time in the season 1980–81?

7. For whom did Neil Fox score a record 6,220 points in a senior Rugby League career spanning the years 1956 to 1980?

8. Which Rugby League club set up the unenviable record of losing forty consecutive league games between 16 November 1975 and 21 April 1977?

9. The International Championship replaced Rugby League's World Cup in 1975. Who won it in that year?

10. In 1975, who became the first winners of the Premiership Trophy?

18.
PEOPLE IN THE BIBLE

1. Who was the elder brother of Moses and Miriam?

2. Whom did God promise, 'Your descendants will be as many as the stars in the sky'?

3. When Absalom's army was defeated in the forest of Ephraim by David's men, what happened to Absalom?

4. Which Roman emperor ordered the census which brought Mary and Joseph to Bethlehem?

5. Who were the parents of King Solomon?

6. In Genesis, who are named as the three sons of Adam and Eve?

7. Who was set free by Pontius Pilate by the wish of the crowd instead of Jesus?

8. What talent of David's took him to the court of King Saul?

9. Why did Herodias want John the Baptist beheaded?

10. Who was given the name 'Israel' by God after an all-night wrestling match with a 'man', and what does the name mean?

11. What occupation did the apostle Matthew follow before he went to join Jesus?

12. Who became leader of the Israelites after the death of Moses?

13. Where was Paul going when he saw a vision of Jesus and was converted to Christianity?

14. Who were the two sons of Jacob and Rachel?

15. What relation was Ruth, whose story is told in the Book of Ruth, to David?

16. Who was crowned King of Judah at the age of eight after the assassination of his father, Amon?

17. What was the apostle Peter's name before Jesus changed it?

18. How old was Methuselah when he died?

19. Whom did the prophet Samuel choose to be first King of Israel?

20. Who, according to the Gospel of Matthew, was ordered to carry Jesus' cross?

19.
PLACES IN BRITAIN

1. What mansion in England is the official country residence of the Prime Minister, and in which county is it situated?

2. Which range of hills extends thirty-five miles along the border between England and Scotland?

3. Where in England can the famous Montagu Motor Museum collection of veteran cars be found?

4. What are the county towns of the following counties: (*a*) Kent (*b*) Surrey (*c*) Shropshire (*d*) Somerset (*e*) Berkshire?

5. Whereabouts in Scotland is the nature-reserve island Ailsa Craig situated?

6. In which of the Potteries towns did Josiah Wedgwood set up his first works in 1759?

7. What were the original cinque ports of England and which two were added later?

8. On which Scottish river does Balmoral Castle stand?

9. Where, according to legend, did Joseph of Arimathea found the first Christian church in England?

10. Which are the largest lakes in (*a*) Northern Ireland (*b*) Scotland (*c*) England?

11. Where is the only mountain railway in Britain?

12. To which Scottish town was the nickname 'Auld Reekie' given because of the curtain of smoke which used to hang over the lower parts of the city?

13. In 1950 the Royal Observatory was moved from Greenwich. Where was it moved to?

14. What place in South Wales is popularly called 'the hole with a mint in it,' and why?

15. In which London cemetery can be found the graves of Michael Faraday, George Eliot and Karl Marx?

16. Which palace is the official residence of the monarch when in Scotland?

17. In which Oxfordshire village was an atomic research station established in 1947?

18. On which Scottish island is Fingal's Cave?

19. By what name is Middlesex Street in London's Whitechapel area better known?

20. In which counties are the following situated: (*a*) Bodmin Moor (*b*) Sherwood Forest (*c*) Dartmoor?

20.
PHILOSOPHY

1. What are the branches of philosophy that concern themselves with: (*a*) beauty and standards of taste (*b*) knowledge and the means of obtaining it (*c*) questions on the ultimate nature of reality (*d*) human conduct and morality?

2. Who was the Greek philosopher who had a philosopher king as the head of an idealized state?

3. Logical positivism was introduced into England in 1936. Who was responsible?

4. Which French thinker/writer popularized existentialism in such novels as *Nausea* and *The Age of Reason*?

5. Who was the brother of a leading American novelist, himself one of the foremost pragmatist philosophers?

6. Who wrote the following: (*a*) *Concept of Mind* (*b*) *Critique of Pure Reason* (*c*) *Principia Mathematica* (*d*) *Treatise of Human Nature*?

7. A thirteenth-century theologian undertook to prove that the thoughts of Aristotle were not contrary to Christianity. Who was he?

8. Who was the leading light in the Vienna Circle, his principal work being *Tractatus Logico-philosophicus*?

9. *'Cogito ergo sum'* ('I think, therefore I am') was a first premise of whom?

10. Leibniz and his followers were caricatured in Voltaire's novel *Candide* by which character?

11. An Anglican bishop, who said that things exist only in being perceived, was dean of Dromore and Derry and, later, bishop of Cloyne. Who was he?

12. A British school of thought had as its 'father' Jeremy Bentham and as its greatest exponent John Stuart Mill. What was it?

13. In his book *Beyond Good and Evil*, which German thinker placed particular emphasis on an élite of supermen?

14. Who was the logician and theologian who secretly married one of his pupils and was subsequently castrated by her family?

15. What was the name given to a group of French thinkers of the eighteenth century which included the Marquis de Condorcet and Voltaire?

16. Which English philosopher was jailed for his pacifist views in the First World War and was later involved in the Campaign for Nuclear Disarmament?

17. His *Essay Concerning Human Understanding* (1690) set British philosophy firmly on a course of empiricism. Who was he, and why was he forced into going abroad in 1683?

18. What is the school of philosophy that took its name from the Greek word for wisdom?

19. Which schools of thought were the following connected with: (*a*) Anselm (*b*) Kant (*c*) Hegel (*d*) Thoreau?

20. Dialectical materialism and its influence on history was incorporated into the political theorizing of whom in his book, *Das Kapital*?

21.
POP MUSIC

1. Which three musicians combined to form Cream in the 1960s?

2. What was the first single record to sell over two million copies in Great Britain, and who recorded it?

3. Who made the following albums: (*a*) 'Revolver' (*b*) 'Exile on Main Street' (*c*) 'Blonde on Blonde' (*d*) 'Rumours'?

4. Which artist recorded the song 'In a Broken Dream', and by what name is he better known?

5. What was Billy J. Kramer's backing group called?

6. From which Beatles' songs do the following lines come: (*a*) 'Waits at the window, wearing the face that she keeps in a jar by the door' (*b*) 'Picture yourself in a boat on a river with tangerine trees and marmalade skies' (*c*) 'Dear Sir or Madam, will you read my book' (*d*) 'When I get older losing my hair, many years from now'?

7. Which singer, who later went solo, formed the group, The Tremeloes?

8. Which group had hits with, among others, 'Money, Money, Money', 'Dancing Queen' and 'Waterloo', and from which country do they come?

9. By what names are (*a*) Reg Dwight and (*b*) Priscilla White better known?

10. With which song did Sandie Shaw win the Eurovision Song Contest for Britain in 1967?

11. Which group was formed in 1962 in Manchester by the combination of two groups, The Deltas and The Dolphins?

12. Who had hits with the following singles: (*a*) '24 Hours from Tulsa' (*b*) 'I'm Mandy, Fly Me' (*c*) 'Waterloo Sunset' (*d*) 'Nights in White Satin' (*e*) 'Bohemian Rhapsody'?

13. Which actor recorded the hit single 'MacArthur Park'?

14. Whose hits have included 'Satisfaction', 'Paint it Black' and 'Jumpin' Jack Flash'?

15. Which group was formed by three brothers, Barry, Maurice and Robin Gibb?

16. Who wrote the following songs: (*a*) 'Mr Tambourine Man' (*b*) 'Candle in the Wind' (*c*) 'World Without Love' (*d*) 'Trains and Boats and Planes'?

17. Which two artists teamed up in 1976 to record the single 'Don't Go Breaking My Heart'?

18. Who was the original lead-singer with Manfred Mann?

19. What is the name of Gladys Knight's backing group?

20. Complete the following names of pop groups: (*a*) Steve Harley and ... (*b*) Siouxsie and ... (*c*) Wishbone ... (*d*) Bob Marley and ... (*e*) Spandau ...?

22.
PEOPLE IN HISTORY

1. Who is the only Englishman to have been made Pope, and what name did he take as Pope?

2. Which French reformation leader wrote *The Institutes of the Christian Religion*?

3. Who were the three husbands of Mary, Queen of Scots?

4. Why was the Duke of Northumberland executed in 1553?

5. Who was the English nun, called the Maid of Kent, who was executed for treason for uttering 'prophecies' denouncing Henry VIII's proposed divorce of Catherine of Aragon?

6. To what position was Robert Devereux, Earl of Essex, appointed by Queen Elizabeth I in 1599?

7. Who was the leader of the Kentish rising against Henry VI in 1450, and what happened to him?

8. Which pretender to the English throne was crowned Edward VI in Dublin Cathedral on 24 May 1487 and later became a falconer in the royal household of Henry VII?

9. Who was dictator of Cuba who was overthrown by Fidel Castro in 1958?

10. Which Welsh chieftain led an unsuccessful revolt against Henry IV in Wales in 1400–13?

11. Who conquered Sicily and Naples in 1860, helping to make Victor Emmanuel King of Italy, and what name was given to his volunteer troops?

12. Which suitor of Queen Elizabeth I was created Earl of Leicester in 1564?

13. Who was captain of the *Bounty* during the mutiny of 1789?

14. Why did Paul Revere make his famous ride in 1775?

15. Who was Commander-in-Chief of the New Model Army who defeated King Charles I in the English Civil War?

16. What did Perkin Warbeck declare himself to be on 7 September 1497?

17. Who carried out Oliver Cromwell's dispossession of the Irish as Lord Deputy of Ireland in 1650?

18. What nickname was given to Ivan IV, Tsar of Russia?

19. Which chief minister of Britain was described as 'my pygmy' by Queen Elizabeth I, and later as 'my little beagle' by King James I?

20. What was the 'Popish Plot' to which Titus Oates testified in 1678?

23.
SOCCER

1. Johann Cruyff has been voted European Footballer of the Year three times when playing for two different clubs. Which clubs?

2. The English Football League Cup was first contested in the 1960–61 season. Who were the winners and whom did they beat in the final?

3. The winners of which two European competitions contest the European Super Cup?

4. The 1970 FA Cup final was the first to be held at Wembley to go to a replay. Which two teams were involved and what was the final result?

5. Where were the World Cup finals held in: (*a*) 1978 (*b*) 1970 (*c*) 1962?

6. In 1981 Liverpool became the first English club to win the European Cup three times. Whom did they beat in that year's final and what was the score?

7. Which were the first English clubs to win the following: (*a*) European Cup (*b*) European Cup-Winners' Cup (*c*) Inter-City Fairs Cup (*d*) European Super Cup?

8. What was unusual about the two goals scored by Tommy Hutchison in the 1981 FA Cup Final?

9. Which famous London football club was called Dial Square when it was founded in 1886?

10. Who was the first European Footballer of the Year when it was instituted in 1956, and for whom did he play?

11. To which countries do the following soccer clubs belong: (a) Boca Juniors (b) Juventus (c) Benfica (d) Red Star Belgrade (e) Feijenoord (f) Borussia Moenchengladbach?

12. For which two English clubs did Sir Matt Busby play soccer in the 1930s?

13. Which club won the European Cup five times between 1955 and 1960?

14. When was the Premier Division introduced into the Scottish League, and how many clubs does it comprise?

15. Which clubs play at the following grounds: (a) Racecourse Ground (b) Meadow Lane (c) Molineux (d) Ayresome Park (e) Gigg Lane (f) Craven Cottage?

16. Who set up a world record by playing in seventy consecutive internationals for England between 1951 and 1959?

17. What was the major difference made to the English League Cup final in the 1966–7 season?

18. Who scored a record thirteen goals in the 1958 World Cup finals in Sweden?

19. What distinction is common to Preston North End, Aston Villa, Tottenham Hotspur and Arsenal?

20. To which clubs do the following nicknames apply: (*a*) Gunners (*b*) Toffeemen (*c*) Trotters (*d*) Magpies?

24.
EXPLORATION AND DISCOVERY

1. Who discovered the Victoria Falls, Lake Nyasa and the Upper Congo?

2. In which year did Robert Scott reach the South Pole?

3. Who was the first man to sail around southern Africa and establish trade links with the Far East?

4. Under whose patronage did Christopher Columbus make four voyages, discovering America while on them?

5. Who was the Frenchman who was the first to navigate the St Lawrence river in Canada?

6. Whose tomb was discovered by Howard Carter and the Earl of Caernarvon in 1922?

7. Who discovered Newfoundland and Nova Scotia in the fifteenth century, believing them to be part of Asia?

8. What part did the Treaty of Tordesillas of 1494 play in exploration?

9. Whose expedition charted the Antarctic continent in 1773–4?

10. Which nineteenth-century American explorer and politician was nicknamed 'Pathfinder'?

11. In 1583 who claimed Newfoundland for England, and what happened to him on the voyage home?

12. Who explored the mouth of the Amazon in 1499 and also proved that South America was not part of Asia?

13. What expedition did Sir Vivien Fuchs lead in 1957–8?

14. In 1576–8, which English mariner made three unsuccessful expeditions in search of the Northwest Passage, and seven years later joined Sir Francis Drake in the West Indies expedition?

15. Who led the Spanish expedition which was the first to circumnavigate the world, and what nationality was he?

16. Which coast did Vasco da Gama reach after rounding the Cape of Good Hope in 1497?

17. Why did Thor Heyerdahl construct a raft of logs, held together by rope, and, with a few companions, sail from Peru to Tuamotu Islands in the South Pacific; and what was his raft called?

18. On which ship did Charles Darwin sail as a naturalist, surveying South America, between 1831 and 1836?

19. Who discovered Lake Tanganyika in 1858?

20. What was the name of the ship in which Francis Drake sailed in 1577 to find a south-west route to Asia?

25.
QUOTATIONS

1. Which US President's mother said: 'I love all my children, but some of them I don't like'?

2. What did General Omar Bradley describe as 'The wrong war, at the wrong place, at the wrong time and with the wrong enemy'?

3. Which US President said: 'There is one thing about being President – nobody can tell you when to sit down'?

4. What did Winston Churchill describe as 'A splendid moment in our great history and in our small lives'?

5. Who wrote: 'The great masses of the people ... will more easily fall victims to a great lie than to a small one'?

6. To what was James VI of Scotland and I of England referring when he said: 'A branch of the sin of drunkenness, which is the root of all sin'?

7. From which Shakespeare plays do the following lines come: (*a*) 'Out, damned spot! out, I say!' (*b*) 'Cry "Havoc" and let slip the dogs of war' (*c*) 'The lady doth protest too much, methinks' (*d*) 'It is a wise father that knows his own child'?

8. At which battle did Horatio Nelson say: 'Before this time tomorrow I shall have gained a peerage or Westminster Abbey'?

9. Which famous actress was quoted as saying: 'I never hated a man enough to give him his diamonds back'?

10. What was the occasion on which Martin Luther King made a speech in which he said: 'I have a dream today . . .'?

11. Whom did Aneurin Bevan describe as 'a man suffering from petrified adolescence'?

12. What did Mme Roland say on passing a statue of 'Liberty' on her way to the scaffold in 1793?

13. Whom was Oscar Wilde referring to when he said: 'He hasn't an enemy in the world, and none of his friends like him'?

14. After which event did Napoleon Bonaparte say: 'From the sublime to the ridiculous there is only one step'?

15. Who said: 'Had I but served God as diligently as I have served the King, He would not have given me over in my grey hairs', and to which king was he referring?

16. What caused Sir Isaac Newton to say: 'Oh, Diamond! Diamond! Thou little knowest the mischief done!'?

17. Whom did Lady Caroline Lamb describe as 'Mad, bad and dangerous to know'?

18. What event occasioned Admiral Yamamoto of the Japanese Navy to say: 'I fear we have only awakened a sleeping giant and his reaction will be terrible'?

19. Which American president said in his inaugural address: 'Ask not what your country can do for you; ask what you can do for your country'?

20. Who was the royal princess who said: 'When I appear in public people expect me to neigh, grind my teeth, paw the ground and swish my tail – none of which is easy'?

26.
ART AND ARTISTS

1. Which British painter left nearly 300 paintings and 20,000 watercolours and drawings to the nation when he died in 1851?

2. Who painted the following: (*a*) *Dedham Vale* (*b*) *Mona Lisa* (*c*) *The Yellow Cornfield*?

3. What was eliminated from the 'rainbow palette' which was devised by Renoir?

4. To which religious order did the artist Fra Angelico belong?

5. Who is best known for his series of paintings of the outlaw Ned Kelly and of the Australian outback?

6. What nationality were the following: (*a*) Bellini (*b*) Bonnard (*c*) Hieronymus Bosch (*d*) Albrecht Dürer?

7. Which fifteenth-century artist painted the *Birth of Venus* and *Primavera*?

8. Who recorded atrocities committed by French troops under Joseph Bonaparte in Spain in a series of etchings called *The Disasters of War*?

9. Which nineteenth-century artist rejected western civilization and went to live in Tahiti?

10. What do the initials P R B stand for, and after whose signature did they first appear at an exhibition in 1848?

11. Who was Michelangelo's patron until 1492?

12. In which year did Picasso die?

13. What was the original meaning of a cartoon?

14. Which nineteenth-century French artist was much influenced by dance halls and cafés in Montmartre such as the Moulin Rouge?

15. Who painted *Les Demoiselles d'Avignon* ('The Maids of Avignon'), one of the first major works of the Cubist movement?

16. Who painted his mother as the Prophetess Hannah?

17. What were the Christian names of the following: (*a*) Cézanne (*b*) Constable (*c*) Degas (*d*) Gainsborough (*e*) Matisse (*f*) Monet?

18. Whose real name was Donato di Niccolo de Betto?

19. Whom did James Whistler sue in 1878 for describing his painting, *Nocturne in Black and Gold*, as 'flinging a pot of paint in the public's face', and how much did the artist receive in damages?

20. Whose free-standing sculpture, *Bronze Age*, was so lifelike and accurate in proportion and anatomy that it gave rise to the tale that it had been made from a cast taken from a live model?

27.
HISTORICAL EVENTS

1. Where in America did the Pilgrim Fathers land from the *Mayflower* in December 1620?

2. When was the Penny Post started in Britain?

3. The Stone of Scone was used for the crowning of Scottish kings until 1296. Which English king stole it and moved it to Westminster Abbey?

4. Where did the Boxer Rising take place in 1897–8?

5. Why was the Hudson's Bay Company formed in Britain in 1670?

6. In what year did India gain independence from Britain?

7. What happened at St Peter's Field, Manchester, on 19 August 1819?

8. What name was given by the Whigs to the Court party formed in Britain by Sir Thomas Danby under King Charles II?

9. Two presidents and a prime minister were involved in talks at Camp David, Maryland, USA, in September 1978. Who were they?

10. In 1859, where in America did John Brown make a raid on a military arsenal?

11. What was the purpose of the Council of Trent which was held from 1545 to 1563?

12. What name was given to the executive power in France between August 1795 and November 1799?

13. What was the Chartist Movement of the 1840s?

14. Which war was ended by the Treaty of Vereeniging?

15. What was the Dogger Bank Incident of 21 October 1904?

16. Which movement was led in England in 1839 by Richard Cobden and John Bright?

17. What was the Great Trek of 1836–7?

18. Which North African country was seized by French troops on 5 July 1830 to avenge a national insult?

19. Where was the Armistice between Germany and the Allied and Associated Powers signed on 11 November 1918?

20. What was ended by the Treaty of Nanking in 1842?

28.
GENERAL KNOWLEDGE (III)

1. Which novelist popularized the terms 'U' and 'non-U' which were introduced into Britain by Professor Alan Ross?

2. What is a theodolite used for?

3. Where is Alhambra, the ancient palace of the Moorish kings which was built in the thirteenth and fourteenth centuries, sited?

4. What are the Elgin Marbles?

5. Which agency of the United Nations Organization was established at the Bretton Woods Conference of 1944?

6. After whom have the following months of the year been named: (*a*) January (*b*) June (*c*) March (*d*) July?

7. In darts, what is the name of the mark from where the throw is taken?

8. What are the two official languages of South Africa?

9. Which English author of books on style and usage wrote *Dictionary of Modern English Usage*?

10. What were the three ages into which prehistory was divided by Danish archaeologist Christian Thomsen?

11. Which national newspaper was founded in 1785 as the *Daily Universal Register*?

12. Who was the 'knight of the doleful countenance' in a novel by Miguel de Cervantes?

13. What are the collective nouns for the following: (*a*) Owls (*b*) Turkeys (*c*) Crows (*d*) Peacocks?

14. Which is the premier order of knighthood in Great Britain?

15. When is Thanksgiving Day celebrated in America, and who instituted this festival?

16. What is a 'wadi'?

17. Before President Kennedy's death, how many previous US presidents had been assassinated?

18. Which day of the week derived its name from Odin, the Norse God of War?

19. During the American Civil War who were the Commanders-in-Chief of (*a*) the Confederate Army (*b*) the Union Army?

20. Which was the last planet to be discovered, its existence being established in 1930 by C. W. Tombaugh?

29.
MEDICINE AND SCIENCE

1. What is the more common name for methane gas?

2. Who discovered the law of gravitation and explained the motion of the planets around the sun?

3. What is 'cryo-surgery'?

4. Who introduced chloroform as an anaesthetic in Britain in 1847?

5. What conditions are caused by a lack of (*a*) Vitamin C (*b*) Vitamin D (*c*) Vitamin B1 (thiamine)?

6. To whom is the first use of the magnifying power of lenses to form a telescope attributed?

7. What is 'acupuncture'?

8. Which English chemist and physicist was the originator of the theory of the atom as the centre of force?

9. For what is the word 'laser' an acronym?

10. Who founded a training school for nurses at St Thomas's Hospital, London, in 1861?

11. Which German bacteriologist, renowned for his work in im-

munology, was joint winner of the Nobel Prize for Medicine and Physiology in 1908?

12. What is 'alopecia'?

13. Who, in around 1592, invented the thermometer?

14. What did the Scottish scientist Sir James Dewar invent in 1892?

15. Which compound is used in medicine to encase broken bones?

16. What are the following more commonly known as: (*a*) Sodium chloride (*b*) Sodium carbonate decahydrate (*c*) Sodium hydroxide?

17. Which French mathematician and physicist climbed a mountain to establish that atmospheric pressure decreases with height?

18. What is caused by the refraction of sunlight through raindrops?

19. After whom is the SI unit of energy named?

20. Which British scientist, who died in 1844, produced an atomic theory of matter which provided the foundation of modern science?

30.
GEOGRAPHY
OF THE WORLD

1. In which countries are the following ports: (*a*) Abadan (*b*) Haifa (*c*) Bergen (*d*) Casablanca?

2. Which is the largest inland sea in the world?

3. What are the capitals of the following European countries: (*a*) Belgium (*b*) Romania (*c*) Sweden (*d*) Denmark (*e*) Norway (*f*) Hungary?

4. Which small, independent state on the Franco-Spanish frontier is under the joint suzerainty of the President of France and the Spanish Bishop of Urgel?

5. Which is the highest volcano in Europe?

6. In which countries can the following waterfalls be found: (*a*) Angel Falls (*b*) Sutherland (*c*) Niagara?

7. Which park and fashionable district in west Paris, given to the city by Napoleon III when he became emperor, contains the racecourses of Auteuil and Longchamp?

8. What were the former names of the following: (*a*) Malawi (*b*) Mali (*c*) Belize?

9. Which two countries do (*a*) the Bering Strait and (*b*) the Palk Strait divide?

10. Dar-es-Salaam is the capital and chief seaport of Tanzania. What does its name mean in Arabic?

11. Which is the largest, most populous continent in the world?

12. What are the capitals of the following South American countries: (*a*) Uruguay (*b*) Brazil (*c*) Paraguay (*d*) El Salvador (*e*) Venezuela?

13. Which two countries comprise the Iberian peninsula?

14. In which country might you experience a 'willy-willy'?

15. Which two oceans do (*a*) the Suez Canal and (*b*) the Panama Canal connect?

16. Mount Everest is the world's highest mountain. Which is the second highest?

17. In which countries are the following lakes: (*a*) Michigan (*b*) Great Slave (*c*) Eyre?

18. Which is the largest ocean in the world?

19. What are the capitals of the following countries: (*a*) New Zealand (*b*) USSR (*c*) Iraq (*d*) China (*e*) Egypt?

20. Which is the highest mountain in Japan?

31.
POETS AND POETRY

1. In which country was T. S. Eliot born and what do his initials stand for?

2. Who wrote the following: (*a*) 'The Listeners' (*b*) 'The Love Song of J. Alfred Prufrock' (*c*) 'The Tiger'?

3. How many lines are there in a sonnet?

4. Who wrote the following lines and what was the name of the poem: 'Fair stood the wind for France, when we our sails advance, nor now to prove our chance, longer will tarry'?

5. What was the lifetime career of Gerard Manley Hopkins?

6. In 1798, which two famous poets produced a volume of poetry called *Lyrical Ballads*?

7. Whose full name was Publius Vergilius Maro?

8. Which poet has also written several murder mysteries under the pseudonym of Nicholas Blake, creating the character Nigel Strangeways?

9. Who, in 1878, walked to Balmoral to try to present a copy of his verse to the Queen?

10. Why was the poet Richard Lovelace imprisoned by the English Parliament for seven weeks in 1642?

11. Whose first book of poems, *Songs of Childhood*, was published under the pseudonym of Walter Ramal?

12. What nationality were the following: (*a*) Baudelaire (*b*) Dante (*c*) Goethe (*d*) Longfellow?

13. Who wrote a poem about the Irish Easter Rebellion called 'Easter 1916'?

14. In 1956 which American poet wrote *Howl and Other Poems* as a protest against society's effect on the 'beat' generation?

15. In which poem does the following line appear and who wrote it: 'Far from the madding crowd's ignoble strife . . .'?

16. Who is best known for his collection of lyric poems, *A Shropshire Lad*?

17. Which English poet first gained recognition with *The Ring and the Book*?

18. Who, in remorse for fancied neglect, buried with the body of his wife, Elizabeth Siddal, the manuscript of poems he had been preparing for press?

19. What did W. H. Auden's initials stand for?

20. Under what pseudonym is the Scottish poet Christopher Murray Grieve better known?

32.
FAMOUS
SPORTING NAMES

1. In 1975 who became the first coloured tennis player to win the men's singles title at Wimbledon?

2. Why was Cassius Clay deprived of his world heavyweight title in 1967?

3. In which sports do or did the following women take part: (*a*) Gillian Gilks (*b*) Ann Packer (*c*) Lyudmila Tourischeva (*d*) Dorothy Hamill (*e*) Margaret Court (*f*) Annemarie Proll?

4. In which sports do or did the following men take part: (*a*) Ed Moses (*b*) Cliff Thorburn (*c*) Peter May (*d*) Lee Trevino (*e*) Stan Mellor (*f*) Roscoe Tanner?

5. Which American tennis player was known as 'Little Mo'?

6. Who became the first bowler to take 300 Test wickets in English cricket?

7. Which countries do the following jockeys come from: (*a*) Yves Saint-Martin (*b*) Willie Shoemaker (*c*) Scobie Breasley?

8. In 1956 who, at the age of twenty-one, became the youngest man to win the world heavyweight boxing championship?

9. Which Englishman held the World Professional Championship in billiards from 1928 to 1930 and again in 1932, and in snooker from 1927 to 1940 and again in 1946?

10. How many times in succession had Bjorn Borg won the men's singles title at Wimbledon before his defeat in 1981, and who finally beat him?

11. Which famous cricketer is known as 'Big Bird', and for which national side does he play?

12. What do the following have in common and from which countries do they come: (*a*) Denny Hulme (*b*) Emerson Fittipaldi (*c*) Nikki Lauda (*d*) Mario Andretti (*e*) Jochen Rindt?

13. In 1979, who won the world speedway championship a record sixth time, and from which country does he come?

14. At which weight did boxer Sugar Ray Robinson become the only boxer to win a world title five times at one weight?

15. In August 1968, which cricketer became the only batsman to score 36 runs off a six-ball over, and for whom was he playing?

16. Who set up a record fourteen Isle of Man TT Race wins between 1961 and 1979?

17. To which boxers have the following nicknames been applied: (*a*) The Manassa Mauler (*b*) Hurricane (*c*) Ambling Alp (*d*) Homicide Hank (*e*) Louisville Lip (*f*) Brockton Blockbuster?

18. Who was the first male tennis player to win all four of the world's major championship singles – Wimbledon, the United States, Australian and French?

19. What are the Christian names of the following jockeys: (*a*) Starkey (*b*) Darley (*c*) Rouse (*d*) Eddery?

20. What are the nationalities of the following cricketers: (*a*) Clive Rice (*b*) Geoff Howarth (*c*) Malcolm Marshall (*d*) Rodney Hogg?

33.
MONARCHS

1. Who succeeded to the English throne at the end of the Wars of the Roses in 1485?

2. In which castle was Edward the Martyr said to have been murdered and Edward II imprisoned after his deposition?

3. Who succeeded to the British throne following the abdication of Edward VIII in 1936?

4. How did Albert I, King of the Belgians, die in 1934?

5. Who, on his deathbed, said 'Let not poor Nelly starve', and who was the Nelly he was referring to?

6. Which grandson of Alfred the Great was crowned king of England in AD 925, becoming the first ruler of all England?

7. Where was Elizabeth I staying when she heard news of her accession to the throne of England?

8. Who was the last Stuart monarch of Britain, and which house took over the monarchy on her death?

9. Which French queen was the mother of three kings of France – Francis II, Charles IX and Henry III?

10. When was the title, Emperor or Empress of India, first added to the monarch's title in Britain, and who was the first monarch to hold it?

11. Which queen of England was known as 'Empress Maud'?

12. Who was the son of Malcolm II who ruled in Scotland from 1040 to 1057 and who did he kill to take the crown?

13. When did Queen Elizabeth II become Queen of England and when was she crowned?

14. Who, on ascending the throne of Britain, made the resolution 'I will be good'?

15. What was the Bill of Rights which William III of Britain was forced to accept in 1689?

16. Who were the parents of the boy king of England, Edward VI?

17. The marriage of which two monarchs united the two kingdoms later known as Spain?

18. Which king reigned in Britain during the American War of Independence?

19. Whom did Queen Mary I of England marry in 1554?

20. Which Queen's last words were: 'All my possessions for a moment of time'?

34.
POLITICS
AND POLITICIANS

1. The first national referendum ever held in the UK took place on 5 June 1975. What was the issue in question?

2. Which Liberal Prime Minister of Britain tried and failed to introduce a Home Rule Bill for Ireland in 1886 and again in 1893?

3. For what post does a British MP apply when he or she wishes to retire from Parliament?

4. Who, in 1917, became the last non-communist Prime Minister of Russia and for how long did he stay in office?

5. What name is given to the Parliament in the Isle of Man?

6. Who was the first American Ambassador to Britain and what did he become in 1797?

7. Why did Scotland and Wales go to the polls on 1 March 1979?

8. Which Norwegian politician became puppet leader of his country during the German occupation in the Second World War, and what happened to him in 1945?

9. In what year did General Franco become head of state in Spain and when did he die?

10. Who was appointed Minister of Labour in Britain in 1940 although he was not then an MP?

11. What action by the House of Lords led to a prolonged constitutional crisis in Britain in 1909?

12. Who was dictator of Portugal for thirty-six years from 1932?

13. Which future British Prime Minister said in his maiden speech to the House of Commons: 'Though I sit down now, the time will come when you will hear me'?

14. Who was communist leader of Yugoslavia from 1945 until his death in 1980?

15. Which political party was formed in Britain in 1981?

16. Who became Prime Minister of Malawi in 1963 and President in 1966?

17. What was the 'Cat and Mouse Act' which was introduced by the Liberal Government in Britain in 1913?

18. Which Ceylonese Prime Minister was assassinated in 1959?

19. Who, in 1977, told a Labour Party Conference: 'Either back us or sack us'?

20. After the 1922 split of Sinn Fein, who headed the Irish Free State government for the next ten years?

35.

GENERAL LITERATURE

1. Which novel by Daphne Du Maurier opens with the line: 'Last night I dreamt I went to Manderley again'?

2. In which of Jane Austen's novels do the following characters appear: (*a*) Darcy (*b*) Mrs Dashwood (*c*) John Knightley?

3. Who created the characters Archdeacon Grantly and Mrs Proudie?

4. In 1888 who completed the first unexpurgated translation of *A Thousand and One Nights*?

5. Who wrote the following: (*a*) *Robinson Crusoe* (*b*) *King Solomon's Mines* (*c*) *The Mayor of Casterbridge* (*d*) *The Hound of the Baskervilles* (*e*) *Madame Bovary*?

6. Whose masterpiece was the eight-part novel *À la recherche du temps perdu*, translated into English as *Remembrance of Things Past*?

7. The following line has become proverbial; who wrote it and what is the name of the work it comes from: 'Oh, East is East, and West is West, and never the twain shall meet'?

8. In which of Thackeray's novels does the heroine Becky Sharp appear?

9. Who wrote the following plays: (*a*) *She Stoops to Conquer* (*b*) *School for Scandal* (*c*) *Lady Windermere's Fan*?

10. Which imaginary country was created by Anthony Hope in his novel *The Prisoner of Zenda*?

11. Who, inspired by a tour of Europe, wrote *The History of the Decline and Fall of the Roman Empire*?

12. What was the name of Bertie Wooster's manservant in stories by P. G. Wodehouse?

13. Who aided the patriot cause in the American Revolution with pamphlets which included *Common Sense*, and later defended the French Revolution in *The Rights of Man*?

14. In which of Charles Dickens's novels do the following characters appear: (*a*) Mr Micawber (*b*) Simon Tappertit (*c*) Tiny Tim (*d*) Bill Sikes?

15. What was the occupation of Mr Lewisham in H. G. Wells's *Love and Mr Lewisham*?

16. Who wrote the following science-fiction novels: (*a*) *The Time Machine* (*b*) *Dune* (*c*) *Twenty Thousand Leagues Under the Sea*?

17. Who wrote the children's classics *Little Women* and *Little Men*?

18. In which of Shakespeare's plays do the following characters appear: (*a*) Petruchio (*b*) Bottom (*c*) Touchstone (*d*) Montague?

19. Who, in a novel by Joseph Conrad, sailed aboard the steamship *Patna*, and what was the title of the book?

20. Who wrote the following children's books: (*a*) *Black Beauty* (*b*) *Peter Pan* (*c*) *The Jungle Books* (*d*) *Winnie-The-Pooh* (*e*) *Treasure Island*?

36.
MUSIC AND MUSICIANS

1. The name of the composer of the opera *Hansel and Gretel* is the same as that of a well-known modern-day singer. What is it?

2. Who wrote the music for the following operas: (*a*) *Tristan and Isolde* (*b*) *Don Carlos* (*c*) *The Trojans*?

3. Which American blues singer was known as 'The Empress of the Blues'?

4. What do the following musical terms mean: (*a*) adagio (*b*) forte (*c*) piano (*d*) vivace?

5. Under whose patronage did George Handel settle in England?

6. *Onward, Christian Soldiers* was one of a number of hymns written by which English composer?

7. With which musical instruments are the following normally associated: (*a*) Larry Adler (*b*) James Galway (*c*) Dizzy Gillespie (*d*) Liberace?

8. Who founded a festival theatre at Bayreuth for his own productions?

9. What is 'pizzicato'?

10. What nationality were the following composers: (*a*) Johann Sebastian Bach (*b*) Alexander Borodin (*c*) Gustav Holst (*d*) Anton Bruckner (*e*) Claude Debussy?

11. On which of Shakespeare's plays was Berlioz's opera *Beatrice and Benedick* based?

12. Who wrote the opera *Bastien and Bastienne* when he was twelve years old?

13. What is the English translation of the German *Eine Kleine Nachtmusik*, and who wrote this work for strings?

14. Whose name was originally Israel Baline and where was he born?

15. Who wrote the music for (*a*) the operetta *Bluebeard* and (*b*) the opera *Bluebeard's Castle*?

16. To which historical figure was Beethoven's *Eroica Symphony* originally dedicated?

17. Which operetta by Johann Strauss was filmed in 1955 as *Oh, Rosalinda*?

18. Of which Gilbert and Sullivan operettas are the following the alternative titles: (*a*) *The Peer and the Peri* (*b*) *The Lass That Loved a Sailor* (*c*) *The King of Barataria* (*d*) *The Town of Titipu*?

19. What is a 'nonet'?

20. Which was Beethoven's only opera?

37.
BATTLES

1. Who fought at Bunker's Hill on 17 June 1775?

2. Which American Indian chief led the Sioux at the Battle of Little Bighorn in 1876?

3. Who commanded the Royalist forces at the Battle of Naseby on 14 June 1645?

4. What was described by Winston Churchill as the 'Battle of the Atlantic' in March 1941?

5. Who was mortally wounded aboard the *Revenge* in 1591 while fighting a battle with Spanish ships at Flores in the Azores?

6. What took place at Rorke's Drift on 22–3 January 1879?

7. Where was James IV of Scotland defeated and killed in 1513?

8. Whom did the British defeat at the Plains of Abraham on 13 September 1759, and who commanded the British force?

9. Which two frigates fought off Boston in 1813 during the Anglo-American War?

10. Who commanded the British forces at the Battle of Balaclava on 25 October 1854?

11. Which Egyptian township was the site of two battles in 1942 between British and Commonwealth forces of the 8th Army and the combined German and Italian armies of Marshal Rommel?

12. Who fought at the Battle of Eylau on 8–9 February 1807?

13. Where did Charles Edward Stuart, the Young Pretender, defeat the English on 21 September 1745?

14. Who were defeated at Vicksburg and Gettysburg in 1863?

15. During which siege did the battle of Inkerman take place on 5 November 1854?

16. Where and when did King Henry VII's men defeat the army of King Richard III of England?

17. What major German offensive was started by von Rundstedt on 16 December 1944?

18. During which war of independence did the Battle of Navarino take place on 20 October 1827?

19. When, during the Second World War, did the Battle of Britain take place?

20. Who fought at the Battle of Midway Island on 4 June 1942?

38.

FAMOUS
MEN AND WOMEN

1. Who instituted the Poppy Day appeal for ex-servicemen?

2. What did Sophia Jex-Blake found in London in 1874?

3. Who was the first Governor-General of India, being often regarded as the founder of the British raj?

4. After which Vietnamese communist revolutionary leader was Saigon renamed?

5. What important contribution to sport was made by John Sholto Douglas, eighth Marquess of Queensberry?

6. Henriette Rosine Bernard was a famous French actress. By what stage name was she better known?

7. Which American general was nicknamed 'Old Blood and Guts' by his troops?

8. Between which two towns was the English highwayman Dick Turpin reputed to have made a famous overnight ride?

9. Who described herself as 'The last of the red-hot mommas'?

10. In 1785 who illegally married King George IV while he was still a minor?

11. Why did Sir Anthony Eden resign as Conservative Foreign Secretary in 1938?

12. Which famous playwright is believed to have been born on St George's Day, 1564?

13. Whose last words before she was executed were: 'I realize that patriotism is not enough. I must have no hatred or bitterness towards anyone'?

14. Which famous French singer, who died in 1963, was known as 'The Little Sparrow'?

15. Why was English agriculturist Jethro Tull important to farming?

16. Who described the ballot as being 'stronger than the bullet'?

17. What caused Florence Nightingale to say on her deathbed 'Too kind – too kind'?

18. Which famous English music-hall entertainer was initially billed as George Hoy?

19. Who was associated with the phrase 'Your Country Needs You'?

20. Which international movement was started by Robert Baden-Powell?

39.
SPORTING KNOWLEDGE

1. Which five races make up the English Classics in horse-racing?

2. In golf what are (*a*) a birdie and (*b*) an eagle?

3. Which American speed skater won five gold medals at the 1980 Winter Olympics?

4. In rowing terms, who are Isis and Goldie?

5. At which American race-track is the Kentucky Derby run?

6. In which sports have the following been world champions: (*a*) David Bryant (*b*) Ray Reardon (*c*) Marion Coakes (*d*) Ard Schenk (*e*) Geoff Duke (*f*) Michael Lee?

7. What is the Ivy League in America?

8. Which Queen of England inaugurated the Royal Ascot race meeting, and which King introduced golf to England?

9. In athletics, which five events comprise the women's pentathlon?

10. Who was the 'Crafty Cockney' who won a World Masters' tournament in 1980 and what was the sport?

11. Which two jockeys rode Red Rum on his three Grand National wins?

12. In cricket, which counties were the first to win the following: (*a*) Gillette Cup (*b*) John Player League (*c*) Benson and Hedges Cup?

13. The venue for the 1981 British Open Golf Tournament was one which had not been used for this event for over thirty years. Where was it?

14. Which sport has the greatest number of regular participants in Britain?

15. A boxing match between which two heavyweight boxers on 25 May 1965 lasted under two minutes?

16. The highest innings in cricket made by an England Test team was 903–7 declared, in 1938. Who were the opposing team?

17. Which is the longest cycling race in the world?

18. In which sports are the following trophies contested: (*a*) Ryder Cup (*b*) Thomas Cup (*c*) Stanley Cup (*d*) Wightman Cup (*e*) America's Cup?

19. Which tobogganing club is the home of the Cresta Run?

20. In cricket, which Cup competition did the NatWest Bank Trophy replace in 1981?

40.
GENERAL KNOWLEDGE (IV)

1. What connection is there between Julius Caesar, Archduke Ferdinand of Austria, Mahatma Gandhi and Abraham Lincoln?

2. When did the first direct elections to the European Parliament take place in Great Britain?

3. From which countries do the following golf players come: (*a*) Gary Player (*b*) Severiano Ballesteros (*c*) Tom Weiskopf (*d*) Bob Charles?

4. Who was the Italian electrical engineer who, in 1895, invented the first practical system of wireless telegraphy?

5. How does a boa snake kill its prey?

6. What is the difference between a dromedary and a bactrian type of camel?

7. Where and on which day of the year were the Prince and Princess of Wales married in 1981?

8. Which is the highest-ranking title in the British Army?

9. What were the four freedoms which President Roosevelt said in January 1941 should be the goal of the Allies?

10. Who is the patron saint of children, and on which day of the year does his feast-day fall?

11. How is the date for Easter fixed?

12. In the British Parliament, what is 'Hansard'?

13. Which five books comprise the Pentateuch in the Old Testament?

14. On the Fahrenheit scale, what are freezing and boiling points?

15. What wedding anniversaries do the following represent: (*a*) China (*b*) Pearl (*c*) Diamond?

16. Why did Queen Elizabeth I of England have a medal struck bearing, in Latin, the inscription 'God blew and they were scattered'?

17. What alphabet was introduced by Sir James Pitman?

18. When were the railways of Britain first unified as British Railways?

19. What were the jobs of the following before they became famous: (a) singer Perry Como (b) actor Clark Gable (c) US President Gerald Ford (d) painter Paul Gauguin?

20. According to the Revelation of St John, what is Armageddon?

Answers

1.
GENERAL KNOWLEDGE (I)

1. Edwin Aldrin and Michael Collins.

2. Multiply it by 1.8 and add 32.

3. Northern Lights.

4. (*a*) September (*b*) November.

5. The Panda

6. (*a*) Arthur Askey (*b*) Ken Dodd (*c*) Jim Davidson.

7. The male is the cob and the female the pen.

8. On the moon.

9. The Rosetta Stone.

10. The flora is the plant life and the fauna the animal life.

11. The Three Pyramids of Giza near El Gizeh, Egypt.

12. The European Economic Community or Common Market.

13. The Hague in the Netherlands.

14. (*a*) Franc (*b*) Mark (*c*) Krone (*d*) Drachma (*e*) Escudo.

15. Milton Keynes.

16. Sir Charles Barry.

17. A hot spring which, at intervals, throws a jet of hot water and steam into the air.

18. New Zealand.

19. 1951.

20. Alexandria.

2.
TV AND RADIO

1. (*a*) *Coronation Street*, Pat Phoenix (*b*) *Dallas*, Linda Gray (*c*) *MASH*, Alan Alda (*d*) *When the Boat Comes In*, James Bolam.

2. Robert Wagner and Stefanie Powers.

3. 2 November 1936.

4. *The Archers*. He is played by Bob Arnold.

5. (*a*) David Soul and Paul Michael Glaiser (*b*) Telly Savalas (*c*) Jack Lord.

6. It's That Man Again.

7. Roger Moore and Ian Ogilvie.

8. Lord (John) Reith

9. (*a*) Magnus Magnusson (*b*) Bamber Gascoigne (*c*) Nicholas Parsons.

10. Angela Rippon.

11. *The Professionals*. They are played by Lewis Collins and Martin Shaw.

12. Janet Webb.

13. He is a private eye. He is played by Trevor Eve.

14. Esther Rantzen.

15. *The Good Old Days*.

16. Kenny Everett.

17. The Light and Third Programmes and the Home Service.

18. Brian Murphy and Yootha Joyce.

19. (*a*) *Monty Python's Flying Circus* (*b*) *The Golden Shot* (*c*) *The Fall and Rise of Reginald Perrin* (*d*) *Are You Being Served?* (*e*) *The Two Ronnies* (*f*) *The Muppet Show*.

20. (*a*) *ITMA* (*b*) *The Clitheroe Kid* (*c*) *The Navy Lark* (*d*) *The Jimmy Young Show* (*e*) *The Goon Show*.

3.
UNTIMELY ENDS

1. Christopher Marlowe.

2. He was killed by an arrow while hunting in the New Forest in Hampshire.

3. Savonarola.

4. At the Alamo, fighting for the independence of Texas.

5. He caught a chill while stuffing a chicken carcass with snow to see if the meat would be preserved.

6. Anne Boleyn and Catherine Howard.

7. Jack Ruby.

8. He was killed when his plane crashed near Ndola on the borders of Zambia and Katanga.

9. John Lennon.

10. St Stephen.

11. The Gunpowder Plot.

12. He was stabbed to death in his house by John Felton, a Suffolk gentleman.

13. Mary, Queen of Scots.

14. He died from an arrow wound received while besieging the Castle of Chalus in Limousin, France.

15. Sir Walter Raleigh.

16. He crashed on a motorcycle and died a few days later from his injuries.

17. Hugh Latimer and Nicholas Ridley.

18. He committed suicide a few hours before he was due to be executed in 1946.

19. At Khartoum.

20. He shot himself.

4.
THE OLYMPIC GAMES

1. Steve Ovett in the 800 metres and Sebastian Coe in the 1,500 metres.

2. 400 metres and 800 metres.

3. Athens in 1896 with twelve nations competing.

4. (a) USA (b) New Zealand (c) Trinidad (d) Jamaica (e) Russia.

5. Robin Cousins.

6. He fell shortly before the halfway mark, recovered and went on to win the gold medal.

7. Johnny Weissmuller.

8. Abebe Bikila (in 1960 and 1964) who competed for Ethiopia.

9. (a) Berlin (b) Mexico City (c) Moscow.

10. The decathlon.

11. The ten-kilometre biathlon.

12. Jesse Owens of America.

13. Downhill, slalom and giant slalom.

14. 1908 and 1948.

15. Bob Mathias.

16. The 100 metres. In the 200 metres he was beaten by Pietro Mennea of Italy.

17. (*a*) Grenoble, France (*b*) Innsbruck, Austria (*c*) Lake Placid, New York.

18. He won the boxing heavyweight title on all three occasions, the only man ever to have done so.

19. (*a*) Swimming (*b*) Gymnastics (*c*) Boxing (*d*) Weightlifting.

20. Nadia Comaneci of Romania.

5.
INDUSTRIAL HISTORY

1. The flying shuttle.

2. *The Great Western.*

3. To grind malt and raise the liquor. It replaced a large wheel turned by six horses.

4. The atmospheric steam engine, used to pump water from mines.

5. Joseph Bramah.

6. (*a*) Sir Richard Arkwright (*b*) James Hargreaves (*c*) Samuel Crompton.

7. 1851.

8. Abraham Darby.

9. To transport his goods, canals being safer and cheaper than the roads.

10. Robert Trevithick.

11. The power loom.

12. Rolls and Royce.

13. Across the Severn near Coalbrookdale in Shropshire.

14. 1819.

15. Protesters against the introduction of new machinery who, in 1811, banded together to wreck the machines.

16. Matthew Boulton, owner of an engineering works in Birmingham.

17. A colliery tramway locomotive.

18. To grind its cocoa beans.

19. George Hudson.

20. He invented the puddling and rolling process which enabled vastly increased quantities of iron to replace wood and stone in many areas.

6.
WRITERS

1. Daphne Du Maurier.

2. (*a*) Gilbert Keith (*b*) David Herbert (*c*) Charles Percy (*d*) James Matthew.

3. Joseph Conrad.

4. Emily, Charlotte, Anne and Branwell.

5. George Eliot.

6. Rachel L. Carson.

7. (*a*) Danish (*b*) Irish (*c*) German (*d*) French (*e*) Russian (*f*) Czech.

8. Cassandra.

9. Izaak Walton.

10. She is his great-granddaughter.

11. Samuel Pepys.

12. He was born in India and from 1922 to 1927 was in the Imperial Police in Burma.

13. Agatha Christie.

14. Westminster Abbey.

15. Terence Rattigan.

16. Hector Hugh Munro.

17. Keith Waterhouse and Willis Hall.

18. Albert Camus.

19. Virginia and Leonard Woolf.

20. Sir Arthur Quiller-Couch.

7.
AMERICA AND AMERICANS

1. Alcatraz.

2. (*a*) Little Rock (*b*) Atlanta (*c*) Austin (*d*) Carson City.

3. Lyndon B. Johnson.

4. 1920.

5. Joseph McCarthy.

6. Sierra Nevada.

7. Franklin Delano Roosevelt, who served between 1933 and 1945.

8. The Alamo.

9. (*a*) Kentucky (*b*) Washington (*c*) Vermont (*d*) Utah.

10. Furth, Germany.

11. Cape Kennedy.

12. An American showman and circus owner whose circus was called 'The Greatest Show on Earth'.

13. Pasadena, California.

14. John Edgar Hoover, Federal Bureau of Investigation.

15. Robert (Bobby) Fischer who beat Boris Spassky of the USSR.

16. Yellowstone National Park.

17. Thomas Jackson.

18. US Military Academy.

19. Jesse and Franklin James.

20. Tsar Alexander II of Russia.

8.
TRANSPORT

1. Model-T Ford.

2. James Brindley.

3. A small submersible craft specially equipped for deep-sea scientific exploration.

4. Sir John Alcock and Sir Arthur Brown.

5. The *Nautilus*.

6. He devised the type of road surface which came to be called macadam.

7. The Russian Army Air Corps.

8. Aircraft Transport and Travel Ltd, a British company founded in 1916 and operating a London-to-Paris service by 1919.

9. Outside the House of Commons in London, to help MPs cross the road.

10. Percy Shaw.

11. Amelia Earhart.

12. The first crossing of the English Channel by balloon.

13. Gottlieb Daimler and Karl Benz.

14. British Overseas Airways Corporation (BOAC) and British European Airways (BEA).

15. (*a*) New York (*b*) Paris (*c*) Tokyo.

16. Morris Motors Ltd.

17. Graf von Zeppelin.

18. The Russian TU-144 which made its first flight in December 1968.

19. He became the first man to fly solo round the world.

20. They invented the first practical hot-air balloon in which they made the first manned flight in 1783.

9.
FOOD AND DRINK

1. (*a*) Greece (*b*) Hungary (*c*) Italy (*d*) China (*e*) Russia (*f*) Spain.

2. Seaweed.

3. Chartreuse.

4. A bunch of fresh herbs – usually bay leaf, thyme and parsley – used for flavouring in cooking.

5. Germany – it's a type of sausage.

6. Tequila.

7. (*a*) Italy (*b*) Holland (*c*) Switzerland.

8. Small cubes, squares or triangles of toasted or fried bread, used for garnishing soups and similar dishes.

9. (*a*) Calf (*b*) Deer.

10. They are both aniseed-flavoured cordials used as absinthe substitutes.

11. Rum and brandy.

12. Austria.

13. Holland.

14. The stomach lining.

15. A flavouring for drinks made from pomegranates.

16. Unleavened.

17. Trinidad.

18. (*a*) Cherries (*b*) Plums.

19. Sweden. It's a table of cold foods.

20. (*a*) China (*b*) Italy (*c*) Austria.

10.
RECORD SETTERS

1. Leon Spinks.

2. Leonardo da Vinci's *Mona Lisa*.

3. Sir Malcolm Campbell.

4. Weightlifting.

5. Colonel Thomas Stafford, Commander Eugene Cernan and Commander John Young.

6. Alex Higgins.

7. Rocky Marciano.

8. The Bible.

9. At the age of 17 years 256 days he became the youngest player to appear in an FA Cup Final.

10. Stan Barratt in *The Budweiser Rocket*.

11. *If*.

12. Bobby Charlton.

13. Twenty.

14. They spent the longest time in space – 175 days – and became the most travelled humans of all time with a mileage of more than 56 million miles.

15. Frank Sinatra.

16. Jersey Joe Walcott.

17. Walt Disney.

18. Mark Spitz. Nine (two in 1968 and seven in 1972).

19. Joe Louis.

20. John Creasey.

11.
GREEKS AND ROMANS

1. Philip II, whose son was Alexander the Great.

2. Actium.

3. Mount Parnassus in Greece.

4. Hadrian.

5. The feat of the messenger Pheidippides, who carried news of the Athenian defeat of the Persians in 490 BC from Marathon to Athens.

6. Claudius.

7. (*a*) Troy and Mycenae (*b*) Knossos on the island of Crete.

8. Pompey; he was assassinated in Egypt.

9. (*a*) Herodotus (*b*) Titus Livius (Livy) (*c*) Cornelius Tacitus (*d*) Thucydides.

10. Caracalla.

11. Ptolemy I, Cleopatra.

12. Rubicon (hence the phrase 'crossing the Rubicon').

13. Athens and Sparta.

14. Lepidus and Octavian.

15. (*a*) Aeschylus (*b*) Sophocles (*c*) Aristophanes.

16. Nero.

17. Pericles.

18. Vespasian; the Colosseum.

19. Solon.

20. Constantine.

12.
TWENTIETH-CENTURY LITERATURE

1. (*a*) Richard Llewellyn (*b*) Evelyn Waugh (*c*) Graham Greene (*d*) William Golding (*e*) Frederick Forsyth (*f*) John Fowles.

2. *Life at the Top.*

3. *The Alexandria Quartet* by Lawrence Durrell.

4. Peter Cheney's.

5. (*a*) Brendan Behan (*b*) Joseph Kesselring (*c*) Bernard Shaw (*d*) W. Somerset Maugham (*e*) Noël Coward (*f*) Arthur Miller.

6. *Gentlemen Prefer Blondes* by Anita Loos.

7. *That Uncertain Feeling.*

8. George Orwell.

9. (*a*) *Look Back in Anger* (*b*) *The Entertainer.*

10. *Of Human Bondage.*

11. Henry Higgins.

12. *Hilda Lessways* and *These Twain.*

13. (*a*) *Catcher in the Rye* by J. D. Salinger (*b*) *Brighton Rock* by Graham Greene (*c*) *Lord of the Rings* and *The Hobbit* by J. R. R. Tolkien (*d*) *Catch 22* by Joseph Heller.

14. W. H. Auden and Christopher Isherwood.

15. Enthusiastic admirers of Jane Austen and her novels.

16. Evelyn Waugh. The three books were *Men at Arms*, *Officers and Gentlemen* and *Unconditional Surrender*.

17. *The Rainbow* and *Women in Love*.

18. (*a*) John Buchan (*b*) Anthony Burgess (*c*) Truman Capote (*d*) Agatha Christie (*e*) C. S. Forester (*f*) Peter Benchley.

19. Biggles

20. *Where Angels Fear to Tread*.

13.
MYTH,
LEGEND AND FOLKLORE

1. The Amazons.

2. The cup from which Christ drank at the Last Supper.

3. Atlas.

4. The jackal-headed god who announced the coming of death and presided over embalmings.

5. Bluebeard.

6. A type of family guardian spirit, the name meaning 'fairy woman', who can portend death.

7. (*a*) Dionysus (*b*) Eros (*c*) Poseidon.

8. Dracula – one of the prince's nicknames was Draculea, meaning Son of the Devil or Son of the Dragon.

9. Merlin.

10. A South American kingdom whose streets and palaces were made of solid gold.

11. Midas.

12. (*a*) Vulcan (*b*) Bacchus (*c*) Mars.

13. William Tell.

14. A winged creature with a woman's head and a lion's body.

15. Odysseus.

16. Hallowe'en, 31 October.

17. St Dunstan.

18. The whereabouts of their treasure.

19. (*a*) Hera (*b*) Juno.

20. Twelve.

14.
GENERAL KNOWLEDGE (II)

1. Mandarin (or Northern Chinese).

2. A knot.

3. Pitcairn Island.

4. (*a*) 1961 (*b*) 1969.

5. Greenland.

6. A small rounded hill or mound.

7. 'Peanuts', created by Charles M. Schulz.

8. Earthquake shocks.

9. Garfield Todd.

10. A stalactite grows downwards and a stalagmite grows upwards.

11. Samuel Colt.

12. (*a*) Gosling (*b*) Owlet (*c*) Tadpole (*d*) Codling.

13. Julius Caesar.

14. Lord Haw-haw. At the end of the war he was captured, convicted of treason and hanged.

15. (*a*) South China Sea (*b*) Gulf of Mexico.

16. The bald eagle.

17. The nose of King Henry I of England and the end of his thumb with his arm outstretched.

18. A cosmonaut.

19. (*a*) Green/White/Orange (*b*) Black/Yellow/Red (*c*) Red/White/Red (*d*) Blue/White/Red.

20. Mother Theresa.

15.
NATURAL HISTORY

1. The blackbird and the chaffinch.

2. (*a*) A small wood left or planted as a harbourage for foxes or game (*b*) A small flock or family party of partridges.

3. The cockroach (which is brown and not a beetle).

4. The badger.

5. Small sea fish, particularly sprats.

6. (*a*) Mosses and liverworts (*b*) Reptiles and amphibians (*c*) Fungi (*d*) Ferns and their allies.

7. Africa.

8. The ferret, which is used for hunting rabbits in their burrows.

9. The dormouse.

10. (*a*) A beetle (*b*) A tree fungus.

11. A steep-sided, circular hollow on a mountainside.

12. The speed of wind.

13. From the legend that it once frightened Cardinal Wolsey at Hampton Court.

14. A small stream in the north of England, equivalent to a burn in Scotland.

15. Fawn.

16. The damage done to a tree by deer cleaning velvet off their antlers.

17. The hare.

18. The hornet.

19. (*a*) Butterfly (*b*) Moth.

20. Ermine.

16.
FILMS
AND FILM STARS

1. *Casablanca.*

2. Norma Jean Baker.

3. Mickey Mouse.

4. Trevor Howard and Celia Johnson. It was directed by David Lean.

5. *Tess of the d'Urbervilles*. The film is called *Tess*.

6. *East of Eden*.

7. Greta Garbo.

8. Eric Liddell and Harold Abrahams.

9. (*a*) Michael Cimino (*b*) Woody Allen (*c*) Sir Carol Reed (*d*) John Schlesinger (*e*) Fred Zinnemann (*f*) Otto Preminger.

10. Katherine Hepburn's was *The Lion in Winter* and Barbra Streisand's was *Funny Girl*.

11. Marlon Brando.

12. Lionel, John and Ethel.

13. Marlene Dietrich, who made her debut in *The Blue Angel*.

14. Dustin Hoffman and Robert Redford.

15. *Gone with the Wind*.

16. Jake La Motta, played by Robert de Niro.

17. Paul Newman and Robert Redford.

18. (*a*) Liza Minnelli (*b*) Richard Dreyfuss (*c*) Gene Hackman (*d*) Jane Fonda (*e*) Rod Steiger (*f*) Julie Andrews.

19. Prince Rainier III of Monaco.

20. Steve McQueen.

17.
RUGBY

Rugby Union

1. England and Scotland.

2. (*a*) Cardiff Arms Park (*b*) Murrayfield (*c*) Lansdowne Road.

3. Guy's Hospital RFC.

4. Parc des Princes.

5. (*a*) New Zealand (*b*) South Africa.

6. (*a*) Colin Meads, New Zealand (*b*) Ian McLaughlan, Scotland (*c*) Tony O'Reilly, Ireland (*d*) Don Clarke, New Zealand.

7. Andy Hill.

8. Wales.

9. Billy Beaumont.

10. (*a*) Ireland (*b*) Scotland (*c*) Wales (*d*) England.

Rugby League

1. Hull Kingston Rovers.

2. David Watkins for Salford.

3. Leeds.

4. Wakefield Trinity and Hull.

5. Eric Ashton.

6. Fulham.

7. Bradford Northern.

8. Doncaster.

9. Australia.

10. Leeds.

18.
PEOPLE IN THE BIBLE

1. Aaron.

2. Abraham.

3. Whilst escaping on a mule he was caught by his hair in the branches of an oak. Joab, David's general, killed him against the King's orders.

4. Augustus Caesar.

5. David and Bathsheba.

6. Cain, Abel and Seth.

7. Barabbas.

8. His skill in playing the harp.

9. Because John the Baptist condemned her marriage to Herod Antipas while Philip, her first husband, was still alive.

10. Jacob. It means 'the man who fights with God'.

11. He was a tax collector.

12. Joshua.

13. Damascus.

14. Joseph and Benjamin.

15. His great-grandmother.

16. Josiah.

17. Simon.

18. 969 years old.

19. Saul.

20. Simon of Cyrene.

19.
PLACES IN BRITAIN

1. Chequers in Buckinghamshire.

2. The Cheviot Hills.

3. Beaulieu, Hampshire.

4. (*a*) Maidstone (*b*) Guildford (*c*) Shrewsbury (*d*) Taunton (*e*) Reading.

5. In the Firth of Clyde.

6. Burslem.

7. Hastings, Romney, Hythe, Dover and Sandwich. Winchelsea and Rye were added later.

8. The River Dee.

9. Glastonbury.

10. (*a*) Lough Neagh (*b*) Loch Lomond (*c*) Lake Windermere.

11. On Snowdon, ascending from Llanberis.

12. Edinburgh.

13. The castle at Herstmonceux in East Sussex.

14. Llantrisant, because it has been the home of the Royal Mint since 1968.

15. Highgate, North London.

16. The Palace of Holyroodhouse in Edinburgh.

17. Harwell.

18. Staffa.

19. Petticoat Lane.

20. (*a*) Cornwall (*b*) Nottinghamshire (*c*) Devon.

20.
PHILOSOPHY

1. (*a*) Aesthetics (*b*) Epistemology (*c*) Metaphysics (*d*) Ethics.

2. Plato.

3. Alfred Jules Ayer.

4. Jean-Paul Sartre.

5. William James, brother of novelist Henry James.

6. (*a*) Gilbert Ryle (*b*) Immanuel Kant (*c*) Bertrand Russell, in association with Alfred North Whitehead (*d*) David Hume.

7. Thomas Aquinas.

8. Ludwig Wittgenstein.

9. René Descartes.

10. Dr Pangloss.

11. George Berkeley.

12. Utilitarianism, 'the right action is that which produces the greatest happiness in the greatest number of people'.

13. Friedrich Wilhelm Nietzsche.

14. Peter Abelard.

15. Les Philosophes.

16. Bertrand Russell.

17. John Locke, forced into temporary exile because of his opposition to Charles II.

18. Sophists.

19. (*a*) Scholasticism (*b*) Rationalism (*c*) Idealism (*d*) Transcendentalism.

20. Karl Marx.

21.
POP MUSIC

1. Jack Bruce, Eric Clapton and Ginger Baker.

2. 'Mull of Kintyre' by Wings.

3. (*a*) The Beatles (*b*) The Rolling Stones (*c*) Bob Dylan (*d*) Fleetwood Mac.

4. Python Lee Jackson, better known as Rod Stewart.

5. The Dakotas.

6. (*a*) 'Eleanor Rigby' (*b*) 'Lucy in the Sky with Diamonds' (*c*) 'Paperback Writer' (*d*) 'When I'm Sixty-four'.

7. Brian Poole.

8. Abba, who come from Sweden.

9. (*a*) Elton John (*b*) Cilla Black.

10. 'Puppet on a String'.

11. The Hollies.

12. (*a*) Gene Pitney (*b*) 10 CC (*c*) The Kinks (*d*) Moody Blues (*e*) Queen.

13. Richard Harris.

14. The Rolling Stones.

15. Bee Gees.

16. (*a*) Bob Dylan (*b*) Elton John and Bernie Taupin (*c*) Lennon and McCartney (*d*) Burt Bacharach and Hal David.

17. Elton John and Kiki Dee.

18. Paul Jones.

19. The Pips.

20. (*a*) Cockney Rebel (*b*) The Banshees (*c*) Ash (*d*) The Wailers (*e*) Ballet.

22.
PEOPLE IN HISTORY

1. Nicholas Breakspear, who became Adrian IV.

2. John Calvin.

3. Francis II of France, Henry Darnley and the Earl of Bothwell.

4. For treason in trying to place his daughter-in-law, Lady Jane Grey, on the English throne.

5. Elizabeth Barton.

6. Lord-Lieutenant of Ireland.

7. Jack Cade, who was executed.

8. Lambert Simnel.

9. Fulgencio Batista.

10. Owen Glendower.

11. Giuseppe Garibaldi, his volunteers being called 'Red Shirts'.

12. Robert Dudley.

13. William Bligh.

14. To warn Massachusetts patriots of the advance of British troops at the outbreak of the American Revolution.

15. Sir Thomas Fairfax.

16. King Richard IV of England.

17. Henry Ireton.

18. The Terrible.

19. Robert Cecil, first Earl of Salisbury.

20. An alleged plot that Catholics were planning to murder King Charles II and replace him with his brother.

23.
SOCCER

1. Ajax and Barcelona.

2. Aston Villa who beat Rotherham United.

3. The European Champion Clubs' Cup and the European Cup-Winners' Cup.

4. Chelsea and Leeds. Chelsea won in the replay 2–1.

5. (a) Argentina (b) Mexico (d) Chile.

6. Real Madrid, 1–0.

7. (a) Manchester United (b) Tottenham Hotspur (c) Leeds (d) Liverpool.

8. He scored one for his own side, Manchester City, and the other as an own-goal for his opponents, Tottenham Hotspur.

9. Arsenal.

10. Stanley Matthews, of Blackpool and England.

11. (*a*) Argentina (*b*) Italy (*c*) Portugal (*d*) Yugoslavia (*e*) The Netherlands (*f*) Germany.

12. Manchester City and Liverpool.

13. Real Madrid.

14. 1975, 10.

15. (*a*) Wrexham (*b*) Notts County (*c*) Wolverhampton Wanderers (*d*) Middlesbrough (*e*) Bury (*f*) Fulham.

16. Billy Wright.

17. Before then it had been a two-legged final. In the 1966–7 season it was made a one-match final, staged at Wembley.

18. Just Fontaine of France.

19. They have all achieved the FA Cup and League double.

20. (*a*) Arsenal (*b*) Everton (*c*) Bolton Wanderers (*d*) Newcastle United.

24.
EXPLORATION
AND DISCOVERY

1. David Livingstone.

2. 1912 (January).

3. Vasco da Gama.

4. Ferdinand II and Isabella of Spain.

5. Jacques Cartier.

6. Tutankhamun, boy-king of ancient Egypt.

7. John Cabot.

8. It was a treaty between Spain and Portugal, marking their respective halves of the world for exploration.

9. Captain James Cook's.

10. John Charles Fremont.

11. Sir Humphrey Gilbert. He was drowned on the return voyage.

12. Amerigo Vespucci.

13. The Commonwealth expedition for the first overland crossing of the Antarctic.

14. Sir Martin Frobisher.

15. Ferdinand Magellan, who was Portuguese.

16. The coast of Natal.

17. To test his theory that Polynesia could have been settled by Indians from South America. His raft was called Kon-Tiki.

18. HMS *Beagle*.

19. Sir Richard Burton with John Hanning Speke.

20. *Golden Hind*.

25.
QUOTATIONS

1. President Carter's mother, Lillian Carter.

2. General MacArthur's proposal to carry the Korean conflict into China.

3. Eisenhower.

4. The unconditional surrender of Germany in 1945.

5. Adolf Hitler in *Mein Kampf*.

6. Tobacco.

7. (*a*) *Macbeth* (*b*) *Julius Caesar* (*c*) *Hamlet* (*d*) *The Merchant of Venice*.

8. The Battle of the Nile.

9. Zsa-Zsa Gabor.

10. A civil rights march in Washington DC in 1963.

11. Winston Churchill.

12. 'O Liberty, Liberty, what crimes are committed in your name!'

13. George Bernard Shaw.

14. The retreat from Moscow in 1812.

15. Cardinal Wolsey, about Henry VIII.

16. A dog called Diamond had knocked down a candle and so set fire to some papers which were the almost finished labours of some years.

17. Byron.

18. The Japanese attack on Pearl Harbor in 1941.

19. John F. Kennedy.

20. Princess Anne.

26.
ART AND ARTISTS

1. Joseph Turner.

2. (*a*) Constable (*b*) Leonardo da Vinci (*c*) Vincent van Gogh.

3. Black.

4. The Dominicans.

5. Sidney Nolan.

6. (*a*) Italian (*b*) French (*c*) Dutch (*d*) German.

7. Sandro Botticelli.

8. Goya.

9. Paul Gauguin.

10. Pre-Raphaelite Brotherhood, the initials appeared after Rossetti's signature.

11. Lorenzo de Medici, Il Magnifico.

12. 1973.

13. A full-size drawing for a painting, usually worked out in complete detail, ready for transfer to a wall, canvas or panel.

14. Toulouse-Lautrec.

15. Pablo Picasso.

16. Rembrandt.

17. (*a*) Paul (*b*) John (*c*) Edgar (*d*) Thomas (*e*) Henri (*f*) Claude.

18. Donatello.

19. John Ruskin. He got one farthing in damages.

20. Auguste Rodin.

27.
HISTORICAL EVENTS

1. Plymouth in Massachusetts.

2. 1840.

3. Edward I.

4. China.

5. To exploit the Canadian fur trade.

6. 1947.

7. The Peterloo Massacre in which eleven people were killed in rioting as soldiers broke up a radical political meeting.

8. Tories.

9. President Carter of America, President Sadat of Egypt and Prime Minister Menachem Begin of Israel.

10. Harpers Ferry, West Virginia.

11. To define doctrine and reform abuses in the Roman Catholic Church.

12. *Directoire* (Directory).

13. An English movement for political reform, advocating universal male suffrage, annual parliaments, vote by ballot, etc.

14. The Boer War.

15. An incident during the Russo-Japanese War in which the Russian Baltic Fleet opened fire by mistake on English fishing boats in the North Sea, sinking one trawler and killing two crew-members.

16. The Anti-Corn Law League.

17. A mass migration from Cape Colony of 10,000 Dutch Boers who wished to form new settlements not under British authority.

18. Algeria.

19. In a railway carriage at Compiègne.

20. The so-called Opium War between Britain and China.

28.
GENERAL KNOWLEDGE (III)

1. Nancy Mitford.

2. Measuring angular distances in the vertical and horizontal planes, particularly in surveying.

3. Granada in Spain.

4. A collection of ancient Greek sculptures and architectural fragments got together by the seventh Earl of Elgin and brought to England between 1802 and 1812.

5. The International Monetary Fund.

6. (*a*) Janus (*b*) Juno (*c*) Mars (*d*) Julius Caesar.

7. The oche – the name comes from the Anglo-Saxon word meaning 'groove in the floor'.

8. English and Afrikaans.

9. Henry Fowler.

10. Stone Age, Bronze Age, Iron Age.

11. *The Times*.

12. Don Quixote.

13. (*a*) Parliament (*b*) Rafter (*c*) Murder (*d*) Muster.

14. The Most Noble Order of the Garter.

15. The fourth Thursday in November. It was instituted by the Pilgrim Fathers.

16. A desert watercourse which is usually dry and contains water only occasionally after a heavy rainfall.

17. Three – Abraham Lincoln, James A. Garfield and William McKinley.

18. Wednesday.

19. (*a*) General Robert E. Lee (*b*) General Ulysses S. Grant.

20. Pluto.

29.
MEDICINE AND SCIENCE

1. Marsh gas.

2. Sir Isaac Newton.

3. The use of freezing techniques in surgery.

4. Sir James Simpson.

5. (*a*) Scurvy (*b*) Rickets (*c*) Beri-beri.

6. Roger Bacon.

7. A treatment, widely used in China, involving the insertion of needles into the skin.

8. Michael Faraday.

9. Light amplification by stimulated emission of radiation.

10. Florence Nightingale.

11. Paul Ehrlich.

12. The scientific name for baldness.

13. Galileo Galilei.

14. The vacuum or Thermos flask.

15. Plaster of Paris.

16. (*a*) Table salt (*b*) Washing soda (*c*) Caustic soda.

17. Blaise Pascal.

18. A rainbow.

19. James Prescott Joule, an English amateur scientist.

20. John Dalton.

30.
GEOGRAPHY
OF THE WORLD

1. (*a*) Iran (*b*) Israel (*c*) Norway (*d*) Morocco.

2. Caspian Sea.

3. (*a*) Brussels (*b*) Bucharest (*c*) Stockholm (*d*) Copenhagen (*e*) Oslo (*f*) Budapest.

4. Andorra.

5. Etna.

6. (*a*) Venezuela (*b*) New Zealand (*c*) Canada.

7. Bois de Boulogne.

8. (*a*) Nyasaland (*b*) French Sudan (*c*) British Honduras.

9. (*a*) USA (Alaska) and Russia (*b*) India and Sri Lanka.

10. Haven of Peace.

11. Asia.

12. (*a*) Montevideo (*b*) Brasília (*c*) Asunción (*d*) San Salvador (*e*) Caracas.

13. Spain and Portugal.

14. Australia. It is a tropical cyclone experienced over the north-west of the country, mainly in late summer.

15. (*a*) Atlantic and Indian (*b*) Atlantic and Pacific.

16. K2 (or Mount Godwin-Austen) in North Kashmir.

17. (*a*) USA (*b*) Canada (*c*) Australia.

18. The Pacific.

19. (*a*) Wellington (*b*) Moscow (*c*) Baghdad (*d*) Peking (*e*) Cairo.

20. Fujiyama.

31.
POETS AND POETRY

1. America, Thomas Stearns.

2. (*a*) Walter de la Mare (*b*) T. S. Eliot (*c*) William Blake.

3. Fourteen lines.

4. Michael Drayton in *Ballad of Agincourt*.

5. He was a Jesuit priest.

6. William Wordsworth and Samuel Taylor Coleridge.

7. Virgil.

8. Cecil Day Lewis.

9. William McGonagall.

10. For presenting the Kentish petition for the retention of bishops and the Prayer Book when Parliament had already declared such a petition seditious.

11. Walter de la Mare.

12. (*a*) French (*b*) Italian (*c*) German (*d*) American.

13. W. B. Yeats.

14. Allen Ginsberg.

15. *Elegy Written in a Country Churchyard* by Thomas Gray.

16. Alfred Edward Housman.

17. Robert Browning.

18. Dante Gabriel Rossetti.

19. Wystan Hugh.

20. Hugh MacDiarmid.

32.
FAMOUS
SPORTING NAMES

1. Arthur Ashe.

2. For refusing to be drafted into the US Army.

3. (*a*) Badminton (*b*) Athletics (*c*) Gymnastics (*d*) Ice skating
    (*e*) Tennis (*f*) Skiing.

4. (*a*) Athletics (*b*) Snooker (*c*) Cricket (*d*) Golf (*e*) Horse racing
    (*f*) Tennis.

5. Maureen Connolly.

6. Freddie Trueman.

7. (*a*) France (*b*) America (*c*) Australia.

8. Floyd Patterson.

9. Joe Davis.

10. Five times. He was beaten in the 1981 final by John McEnroe.

11. Joel Garner of the West Indies.

12. They are all former world motor-racing champions. (*a*) New
     Zealand (*b*) Brazil (*c*) Austria (*d*) America (*e*) Germany.

13. Ivan Mauger of New Zealand.

14. Middleweight.

15. Sir Garfield Sobers, playing for Nottinghamshire.

16. Mike Hailwood.

17. (*a*) Jack Dempsey (*b*) Reuben Carter (*c*) Primo Carnera (*d*) Henry H. Armstrong (*e*) Muhammad Ali (*f*) Rocky Marciano.

18. Fred Perry of Great Britain.

19. (*a*) Greville (*b*) Kevin (*c*) Brian (*d*) Pat.

20. (*a*) South African (*b*) New Zealander (*c*) West Indian (*d*) Australian.

33.
MONARCHS

1. Henry Tudor (Henry VII).

2. Corfe Castle, Isle of Purbeck, Dorset.

3. His brother, George VI.

4. He was killed in a mountaineering accident in the Ardennes.

5. Charles II, who was referring to Nell Gwyn.

6. Athelstan.

7. Hatfield manor in Hertfordshire.

8. Queen Anne. The House of Hanover.

9. Catherine de Medici.

10. 1 May 1876, Queen Victoria.

11. Matilda.

12. Macbeth, who killed Duncan I.

13. She became Queen on 6 February 1952 and was crowned on 2 June 1953.

14. Queen Victoria.

15. A Bill establishing the supremacy of Parliament and denying the ruler the right to suspend the laws of the land whenever it suited him.

16. Henry VIII and Jane Seymour.

17. Queen Isabella I of Castile and King Ferdinand of Aragon.

18. George III.

19. King Philip II of Spain.

20. Queen Elizabeth I.

34.
POLITICS
AND POLITICIANS

1. Whether Britain should remain in the Common Market.

2. William Gladstone.

3. Stewardship of the Chiltern Hundreds.

4. Alexander Kerensky, who became Prime Minister in July and was forced to flee the country the following October.

5. The Court of Tynwald.

6. John Adams, who became President of the USA in 1797.

7. To decide on the question of the establishment of separate assemblies for Scotland and Wales.

8. Vidkun Quisling, who was tried and executed for treason in 1945.

9. 1939 and 1975.

10. Ernest Bevin.

11. Its rejection of the Budget.

12. Antonio de Oliveira Salazar.

13. Benjamin Disraeli.

14. Tito (his real name was Josip Broz).

15. Social Democratic Party.

16. Hastings Banda.

17. The 'Prisoners, Temporary Discharge for Health, Act', introduced to provide for the release on licence of suffragettes who refused to take food while in prison. The licence would be revoked if the released prisoner committed a further offence.

18. Solomon Bandaranaike.

19. James Callaghan.

20. William Thomas Cosgrave.

35.
GENERAL LITERATURE

1. *Rebecca.*

2. (*a*) *Pride and Prejudice* (*b*) *Sense and Sensibility* (*c*) *Emma.*

3. Anthony Trollope.

4. Sir Richard Burton.

5. (*a*) Daniel Defoe (*b*) Sir Henry Rider Haggard (*c*) Thomas Hardy (*d*) Sir Arthur Conan Doyle (*e*) Gustave Flaubert.

6. Marcel Proust.

7. Rudyard Kipling in the *Ballad of East and West.*

8. *Vanity Fair.*

9. (*a*) Oliver Goldsmith (*b*) Richard Brinsley Sheridan (*c*) Oscar Wilde.

10. Ruritania.

11. Edward Gibbon.

12. Jeeves.

13. Thomas Paine.

14. (*a*) *David Copperfield* (*b*) *Barnaby Rudge* (*c*) *A Christmas Carol* (*d*) *Oliver Twist*.

15. He was a schoolteacher.

16. (*a*) H. G. Wells (*b*) Frank Herbert (*c*) Jules Verne.

17. Louisa May Alcott.

18. (*a*) *The Taming of the Shrew* (*b*) *A Midsummer Night's Dream* (*c*) *As You Like It* (*d*) *Romeo and Juliet*.

19. Jim in *Lord Jim*.

20. (*a*) Anna Sewell (*b*) J. M. Barrie (*c*) Rudyard Kipling (*d*) A. A. Milne (*e*) Robert Louis Stevenson.

36.
MUSIC AND MUSICIANS

1. Engelbert Humperdinck.

2. (*a*) Wagner (*b*) Verdi (*c*) Berlioz.

3. Bessie Smith.

4. (*a*) slow and leisurely (*b*) loudly (*c*) soft in tone (*d*) lively.

5. King George I.

6. Sir Arthur Sullivan.

7. (*a*) Harmonica (*b*) Flute (*c*) Trumpet (*d*) Piano.

8. Richard Wagner.

9. The playing by plucking with the fingers of instruments such as the violin which are normally played with a bow.

10. (*a*) German (*b*) Russian (*c*) English (*d*) Austrian (*e*) French.

11. *Much Ado About Nothing*.

12. Mozart.

13. 'A Little Night-Music' by Mozart.

14. Irving Berlin who was born in Russia.

15. (*a*) Offenbach (*b*) Bartók.

16. Napoleon.

17. *Die Fledermaus*.

18. (*a*) *Iolanthe* (*b*) *HMS Pinafore* (*c*) *The Gondoliers* (*d*) *The Mikado*.

19. A composition for nine instruments or nine voices.

20. *Fidelio*.

37.
BATTLES

1. The British under General Howe and the Americans under Colonel Prescott.

2. Sitting Bull.

3. Prince Rupert of the Rhine.

4. The struggle for control of vital supply-routes to the British Isles in the Second World War.

5. Sir Richard Grenville.

6. 140 British troops repelled attacks by 4,000 Zulus.

7. Flodden, Northumberland.

8. The French under Montcalm. The British were commanded by General Wolfe.

9. USS *Chesapeake* and HMS *Shannon*.

10. Lord Raglan.

11. El Alamein.

12. The French under Napoleon against the Russians and Prussians under Bennigsen.

13. Prestonpans.

14. The Confederates in the American Civil War.

15. The siege of Sebastopol in the Crimean War.

16. Bosworth, Leicestershire, on 22 August 1485.

17. The Ardennes Offensive, an attempt by the Germans to break through the Allied front in the west and capture Antwerp.

18. The Greek War of Independence.

19. Between 10 July and 31 October 1940.

20. The navies of the US and Japan.

38.
FAMOUS
MEN AND WOMEN

1. Earl (Douglas) Haig.

2. The London School of Medicine for Women.

3. Warren Hastings.

4. Ho Chi Minh.

5. He devised the Queensberry Rules, the basis of modern boxing.

6. Sarah Bernhardt.

7. George Patton.

8. London and York.

9. Sophie Tucker.

10. Maria Anne Fitzherbert.

11. Because of Chamberlain's 'appeasement' of Hitler.

12. William Shakespeare.

13. Edith Cavell.

14. Edith Piaf.

15. He introduced new farming methods, notably inventing the mechanized seed-drill.

16. Abraham Lincoln.

17. She was handed the insignia of the Order of Merit.

18. George Formby.

19. Horatio Kitchener.

20. The Boy Scouts Association.

39.
SPORTING KNOWLEDGE

1. 2000 Guineas, 1000 Guineas, Derby, Oaks and St Leger.

2. (*a*) One shot under par (*b*) Two shots under par.

3. Eric Heiden.

4. The reserve Oxford and Cambridge boat-crews who compete immediately prior to the main Oxford–Cambridge University Boat Race.

5. Churchill Downs at Louisville.

6. (*a*) Bowls (*b*) Snooker (*c*) Show jumping (*d*) Speed skating (*e*) Motor cycling (*f*) Speedway.

7. An athletics conference of American East Coast colleges, including Harvard, Yale and Princeton.

8. Queen Anne and James I.

9. 100 metres hurdles, shot, high jump, long jump and 200 metres.

10. Eric Bristow, darts.

11. Brian Fletcher (in 1973 and 1974) and Tommy Stack (1977).

12. (*a*) Sussex (1963) (*b*) Lancashire (1969) (*c*) Leicestershire (1972).

13. Royal St George's, Sandwich, Kent.

14. Angling.

15. Cassius Clay (later Muhammad Ali) and Sonny Liston.

16. Australia.

17. The Tour de France.

18. (*a*) Golf (*b*) Badminton (*c*) Ice-hockey (*d*) Tennis (*e*) Yachting.

19. The St Moritz Tobogganing Club in Switzerland.

20. The Benson and Hedges Cup.

40.
GENERAL KNOWLEDGE (IV)

1. They were all victims of assassination.

2. June 1979.

3. (*a*) South Africa (*b*) Spain (*c*) USA (*d*) New Zealand.

4. Guglielmo Marconi.

5. By crushing it.

6. A dromedary has only one hump, a bactrian has two.

7. St Paul's Cathedral, London, on 29 July.

8. Field Marshal.

9. Freedom of speech and expression; Freedom of every person to worship God in his own way; Freedom from want; Freedom from fear.

10. St Nicholas, 6 December.

11. It is the first Sunday after the full moon following the vernal equinox.

12. The title given to the official reports of parliamentary debates.

13. Genesis, Exodus, Leviticus, Numbers and Deuteronomy.

14. Freezing point is 32° and boiling point 212°.

15. (*a*) 20th (*b*) 30th (*c*) 60th.

16. To commemorate the defeat of the Spanish Armada.

17. The initial teaching alphabet, devised to make learning to read English easier.

18. 1 January 1948.

19. (*a*) Barber (*b*) Lumberjack (*c*) Male model (*d*) Stockbroker.

20. A great battle in which the final conflict between good and evil is to be fought.